Politics and Web 2.0: The Participation Gap

Edited by

J. Paulo Serra

Gisela Gonçalves

University of Beira Interior

Vernon Series in Politics

VERNON PRESS

www.vernonpress.com

Vernon Press is an imprint of Vernon Art & Science Inc.

In the Americas:
Vernon Press
1000 N West Street,
Suite 1200, Wilmington,
Delaware 19801
United States

In the rest of the world:
Vernon Press
C/Sancti Espiritu 17,
Malaga, 29006
Spain

Library of Congress Control Number: 2016939403

Vernon Series in Politics

ISBN 978-1-62273-108-4

Contents

List of Figures

List of Tables

Chapter 1

Introduction

J. Paulo Serra and Gisela Gonçalves

The starting point of this book is the paradoxical state of the art regarding political communication's potential and pitfalls in the Web 2.0 era.[1] In fact, empirical evidence has shown that neither citizens nor political parties have been taking full advantage of online features in regard to political participation. This is particularly evident in the case of political parties' websites, which have taken on two main functions: i) Disseminating information to citizens and journalists about the history, structure, programme and activities of the party; ii) Monitoring citizens' opinions in regard to different political questions and policy proposals that are under discussion. This means that, in spite of the integration of websites into political parties' "permanent campaigns" (Blumenthal), TV continues to be seen as the core medium in political communication and thus one-way and top-down communication strategies still prevail. In other words, it is "business as usual".

Several issues arise from this context. With this book, we aim to keep the debate around the party-citizen "participation" mismatch alive. Ultimately, we consider it important to inquire as to whether Web 2.0 could help citizens' political participation or if a new research stream should be identified. The chapters of this book respond to that challenge and provide valuable explorations of how political parties face the digital online apparatus regarding citizen participation at micro and macro level. The micro level involves research on an individual level, mainly focusing on the practices of individuals, while the macro level is more aimed at an analysis of broader, inter-societal systems. Within the 6 chapters gathered in this book, both levels of analysis are presented and intertwined, which leads to an overarching and thought-provoking discussion

[1] This was also the theme of the research project "New media and politics: citizen participation in the websites of Portuguese political parties", developed at University of Beira Interior between 2012 and 2015 with a FCT (Foundation for Science and Technology) grant. More information can be found here: `http://www.political-participation-web.ubi.pt/`

about the political participation gap, its causes and consequences for political communication and democratic politics, as well as new forms of political participation in contemporaneity.

The first chapter in the volume critically reflects on the history of communication studies, often focused on the effects of the media, to demonstrate how some characteristics of Web 2.0 provide elements for a communication theory that is able to provide a framework for social changes and the implications of communication processes in social semiosis, i.e. the semiosis of mediatization. In "*In search of a return to communication (studies) as a factor of social change: Web 2.0 and political participation*", Giovandro Marcos Ferreira, from the Federal University of Bahia, Brazil, is concerned with demonstrating the importance of the community, exercising citizenship on and over the internet, and its links with other institutions that are present in the public space. In particular, the author reflects on how the new wider public space can include what are known as "extimate" operations – a play on words that means externalizing the intimate. In other words, it is a space often frequented by emotion, intimacy and passion in public discussions.

Joaquín Lopez del Ramo, from the Universidad Rey Juan Carlos, Spain, presents "*Descriptive indicators of photojournalistic treatment of political leaders from the standpoint of content analysis*". With this research, he uses the content analysis methodology to obtain in-depth, exhaustive and relevant data on how photojournalism deals with political leaders. Moreover, he underlines how stereotypes, ideological bias and an excess or abuse of "clichés", especially during electoral campaigns, may explain the distance between the public and politicians, by broadcasting the impression of a prefabricated image, hollow rhetoric or even falseness.

The Spanish political party *Podemos*, new on the European scene, is the focus of the chapter authored by Karen Sanders, from CEU San Pablo University and the IESE Business School, Spain. In "*The emergence of Spain's Podemos (We Can) Party: Challenges for political communication practice and study*" the author discusses how *Podemos* and other political groups and the popular distrust of mainstream politicians and political parties have placed the phenomenon of political populism firmly on the Spanish political and public agenda. Moreover, the author discusses how *Podemos*' highly professional approach to political communication, using both traditional and social media to great effect, has at the same time sought to democratize its communication. This leads to an interesting debate about the so-called "false dichotomy", according to which professional campaigns are seen as somehow incompatible with democratic communication that empowers the citizen.

The concept of cosmopolitanism and its importance for understanding the modern transnational world is at the core of the chapter by Peter Dahlgren, from Lund University, Sweden, who critically analyses its utility in helping to understand the conditions for political activism in the context of a global civil society. The essay "*Cosmopolitanism, media and global civil society: From moral to political agency*" begins with reflections on global activism and stresses that much of the literature on cosmopolitanism comprises a normative discourse, asserting a moral obligation to global Others. The author then attempts to make the transition from moral to political engagement, and argues for the notion of civic cosmopolitanism.

Evandro Oliveira, from Leipzig University and the University of Minho, together with Gisela Gonçalves, from the University of Beira Interior, centre their research on the Portuguese Parliament's online communication to reflect on how social media is being used to foster interaction and dialogue between citizens and Members of Parliament. In "*Talk to me and I will talk for you*", the authors anchor their research in the sociological context of social media communication and its relationship with online political communication and relationship management studies from a political public relations perspective. The main findings obtained with a multimethod approach suggest that the level of professionalization of MPs' online communication is low and that the internet's dialogical promise has not yet materialized in the Portuguese parliamentary realm.

Completing the volume, "*New media and politics: citizens' participation in the websites of Portuguese political parties: main results*", is a chapter in which J. Paulo Serra and Gisela Gonçalves, from the University of Beira Interior, Portugal, present the main findings and discuss the main results obtained throughout the various stages of the three-year implementation of the "*New media and politics: citizen participation in the websites of Portuguese political parties*" project. It aimed to answer to the question 'What is the degree of correspondence between the participation that the websites of the Portuguese political parties allow citizens and citizens' expectations about their participation in non-electoral periods?". By using multiple methods of data collection and analysis (content analysis, controlled experiments, semi-structured interviews, web-based surveys and focus groups), the authors conclude that there is a degree of total correspondence. However, as they also highlight, this affirmative answer hides a doubly negative one: i) the political parties' websites *do not* provide citizens with real participation, but only a simulation of participation, with persuasive and propagandistic objectives; ii) citizens *do not* expect the political parties' websites to allow them more participation than they already do, since what citizens mainly want from the websites is information about the parties.

Finally, we hope that this volume achieves our main goal: to enrich the debate and open new avenues in the study of political participation and Web 2.0. We thank all the contributors, reviewers and thoughtful critics without whose contributions this book would not have been possible.

The Editors

Chapter 2

In search of a return to communication (studies) as a factor of social change: Web 2.0 and political participation

Giovandro Marcos Ferreira

"The unknown is found at the frontiers of the sciences"
Marcel Mauss

On the standard history of the communication field (on the effects of theory)

Different communication handbooks study a range of approaches with little overlap among them. In general, the smallest core features found in many handbooks are studies on effects. Elihu Katz states in presentations that he does not know what the object of study of communication is, although he knows what his object of study is in the field of communication – effects. When he says this, he somehow reveals the importance that those studies have had throughout his life and for several researchers in the United States and other countries in the world, highlighting part of the history of communication theories.

There is a standard history of communication theories that views communication studies above all from the bias of effects. It sometimes polarizes and reduces the research's past to "the apocalyptic and integrated", as Umberto Eco (1978) put it simply in 1964. This perspective of the history of communication theories departs from parallel studies in the field of communication and focuses on reporting the research of prevailing studies.

It is important to point out the contexts that support this perspective since the USA's preparation to enter the Second World War and, later, the period marked by the Cold War. An important aspect in this *demarche* that consolidates the prevailing paradigm was the Rockefeller Foundation Communication Seminar from September

1939 to June 1940. In a broader sense, it would be interesting and necessary to have more in-depth studies on the influence of foundations (Rockefeller, Ford, etc.) and government bodies on the direction of the communication field, above all as regards the formation of the paradigms that practically monopolize communication handbooks and the institutionalization of this field in universities. The Rockefeller Seminar was led by John Marshall, a director at the Foundation, who defined the event as:

> a gathering with 12 specialists for monthly meetings to form a general theoretical framework that enables the Foundation to define relevant criteria for possible support for research projects in communication (*apud* Proulx, 2010, p. 40-41).

Before the USA joined the Second World War, with the aim of expanding and involving countries in the conflict, the main question that guided the seminar's agenda was "how can the American government use the media to deal with new geopolitics and the possible involvement of the United States in a world war" (*ibid.* p. 41). To some extent, the "fathers of communication" attempted, in their scientific concerns, to meet the need to achieve consensus among the American people on the USA joining the war. As already mentioned, it later continued to respond to similar demands in the climate of the Cold War, and shifted research to mass communication. In the new enemies, it found actions related to propaganda, which is a decreasingly used term in North American academia.

With the advent of the Rockefeller Seminar, a section of communication studies was organized and consolidated by the development of a state project. The most prevalent and ambitious figure, who would take a prominent place in the state organization, was Harold Lasswell, who became Chief of the Experimental Division for the Study of War Time Communications at the Library of Congress, in Washington. In his memoirs, Lasswell writes:

> With the progressive involvement of the United States in the defence effort, my duties as consultant were more focused on projects directly linked to that effort. From 1939 onwards, I was part of an informal group under the aegis of the Rockefeller Foundation to assess the status of research in the mass communication field and studies of public opinion. Based on those discussions,

> the idea of research on war communication grew, and I was invited by the Foundation to submit a project. That was what I did, and I was given two years, which were then extended so I could commit to a programme with three fronts: 1) developing "content analysis" methods in communication research, as well as organizational analysis (such as at the Attorney General); 2) training personnel at government agencies, who were hoped to become more actively involved in propaganda and intelligence services; 3) staying ready, in Washington, so that I could be a kind of consultant for public officials developing different forms of government propaganda and the progress of intelligence (*apud* Varão, 2015, p. 5).

Around the same time, Paul Lazarsfeld, at Columbia University in New York, directed the Bureau of Applied Social Research in partnership with Robert K. Merton. However, it is important to note that Lasswell had a role to play in the area, thanks to the space he occupied in Washington and his creation of a model (who said what, in what medium, to what effect...), which became a prevailing framework for connecting the problems of specialists in mass communication research in the USA. A type of invisible college was formed, which included several researchers who came together in government bodies to work on their own problems and research topics. They included the following people (Rogers, 1997):

- The experimental psychologist Carl Hovland, of Yale University (Yale Psychology Department), was dedicated to assessing propaganda films for North American soldiers, having in mind an extension of the war. On this mission, he moved away from the university to direct the "Soldier Morale" research programme with the Pentagon. Hovland's research is at the origin of the tradition of research projects about persuasion in the field of mass communication.

- The mathematician Norbert Wiener, of the Massachusetts Institute of Technology (MIT), who worked for the Pentagon at the time of the war, working on problems related to weapons aimed at mobile targets. He took his studies to the fields of probabilistic physics, philosophy and neurology, and published a book called *Cybernetics* in 1948. Wiener viewed information as a quantity, from the same perspective as energy or matter. In other words, it was a material that can be studied for its ability to transmit information. Later, from the same perspective, there was a revolution caused by computers and a trend towards cybernetics emerged, in an attempt to connect a communication science to the natural sciences.

- The mathematician Claude Shannon, of the Bell Labs in New York, cooperated during the Second World War with cryptography analysis, and focused on telecommunications studies centred on the problem of encoding and decoding messages. In 1948, he published an important paper called *A Mathematical Theory of Communication*, and in 1949 he published a book co-authored by Warren Weaver, with the same title as the previous article.

- Wilbur Schramm founded the university field of communication studies in the USA, and had a marked influence in establishing communication departments at several North American universities. However, his influence was not limited to the USA. It also reached other continents, with research assessing mass communication and educational reform, television, radio broadcasting, etc. Schramm had a determining influence with the publication of his book *Mass Media and National Development*, in cooperation with UNESCO, which was concerned with connecting the spread of communication technology and socio-economic development (Schramm, 1997).

Wilbur Schramm is important in structuring the field of communication at universities, and his vision about the communication field is also important, especially when he started working at universities in the USA. A significant book in that area is *The Beginnings of Communication Study in America*, published in the USA in 1997, after his death.[1] It is divided into two main parts. In the first part, "The Forefathers of Communication Study in America", Schramm briefly mentions "the Forefathers of Our Forefathers", citing Charley Cooley, Robert Park and Edward Sapir as examples. He then names and introduces the forefathers of communication in

[1] The book was published by Steven H. Chaffee and Everett M. Rogers 10 years after Schramm's death. Schramm, Wilbur (1997). *The beginnings of communication study in America: a memoir*, Thousand Oaks: Sage Publications.

the USA, focusing particularly on 4 founding fathers ("Our Forefathers"): Harold Lasswell, Paul Lazarsfeld, Kurt Lewin and Carl Hovland. He ends with a chapter called "The Heritage They Left Us", which is split into 9 sections: (1) The Rise of Communication Study; (2) The Magnitude of Change; (3) The Challenge to Simplicity; (4) Doubts About Some Old Models: Minimal Effects; (5) Doubts About Some Old Methods; (6) Communication as a Study of Culture; (7) Communication as "Sociology"; (8) A Countermovement From Critical Researchers; (9) Challenge of the Information Age. The second part, "The Establishment of Communication Study in America", is divided by Steven Chaffee and Everett Rogers into two chapters, paying homage to Schramm: (1) Wilbur Schramm: The Founder and (2) Institutionalization of Advanced Communication Study in American Universities, which is essentially Schramm's teaching plan (The Schramm Plan) for different universities.

This explanation is to underline the core of the standard history of communication that is remembered and celebrated by many handbooks found on communication courses, as a type of "this is how our parents did it and this is what they told us". It defines this history as if it were all of the field's past, formed by some problems based on the legacy left behind. The standard history can be described from two perspectives, according to Jefferson Pooley (2008). One is built by sociologists, especially Paul Lazarsfeld and Elihu Katz, and has a fragile but long-lasting method: personal influence. It refers to pre-war academic predecessors as ingénues, uninformed amateurs, who clung to the "hypodermic theory", the "hypodermic needle" and the "magic bullet theory" of the media, still notably influenced by European theorists of the "mass society theory". That view of their predecessors, according to the author, was contrasted by the sophisticated (and reassuring) scientific "limited effects" approach. Furthermore, it was a conscious creation by Wilbur Schramm, a consummate academic entrepreneur, as almost the only person responsible for institutionalizing communication at universities, through his genealogy of the importance of the four founding fathers and his importance in the foundation and academic consolidation of communication.

A more complete and diversified history of mass communication research has yet to be written, and is hoped to do justice to the different contributions made, including researchers from other scientific fields who have enriched the issues raised about the media. The challenges posed by the relevance of the role of the media in today's social dynamics, above all since the advent of Web 2.0, require the creation of new analysis models for a different media scenario. The success of that challenge, which will provide a communication field that is more sustainable in theoretical terms, may be based around some guiding actions. At an initial stage, as mentioned above, this can be done by revisiting the wealth of communication studies made throughout the 20th century, moving beyond the dominant paradigm and better understanding the changes in the technological and socio-cultural background. It should above all identify the weighted trends of the current context and then analyse how meaning is produced based on new communication process methods in an environment marked by mediatization and the revolution in access.

Underlying this challenge, there is another, bound by two contrasting views of the communication field. On the one hand, the history of communication studies is presented in a limited way and, as highlighted above, it is reproduced in many handbooks. On the other hand, the most recent landscape of studies is designed to be a mosaic that approaches "creative chaos", again reproducing two extremes of the same field of study (Sodré, 2012; Ferreira, 2003).

As a field strategy, a hyper-atrophied view should be overcome, as should disconnected diversity in order to develop "strong enough ways for integrating and benefitting from its diversity". Craig Calhoun also says that "communication is the most important field for the study of many key dimensions of social change" (2011, p. 1480). Therefore, if the communication field becomes more rigid, atrophying its history, it will generally offer intellectually conservative paths and evidence, at a time that is relevant and favourable and in a place that is well positioned for analysing contemporaneity.

> The standard historical narrative enabled a certain way of avoiding the political criticism of liberalism by reducing the question of mass media to the issue of whether or not they had an effect on individuals. This spread of questioning in terms of effects impedes a questioning of the phenomenon of mass media as regards the issue of social control in the hands of the elites that hold them (Proulx, 2010, p. 48).

In this era of Web 2.0, with its social networks and new modes of community life, it is probably a good moment to revisit the concepts of communication involved in the process of creating community ties, such as those put forward by John Dewey, Georges H. Mead, Robert Park, Charles Cooely. John Dewey envisages communication as a type of information that allows for experiences to be exchanged, for ideas to be shared. He connects communication and education, and communication is seen as "a process that is the main element to make the connection between members of a society, and is, in fact, a necessity" (Varão & Cunha, 2014, p. 4326).

By connecting communication and education, it is also possible to identify numerous contributions by Latin American thinkers, including Paulo Freire, who intended for his problem-posing education to improve the shifts between "real awarenes" and "possible awareness", which underlies the concept of communication:

> the thinking subject cannot think alone; he cannot think without the participation of other subjects in the act of thinking about the object. There is no "I think" without a "we think". It is "we think" that establishes the "I think" and not the other way round. This co-participation in the act of thinking has a place in communication. It is exactly for this reason that the object is not the last recourse of a subject's thought, but rather the mediator of communication. Therefore, as the content of communication, it cannot be communicated from one subject to another (Freire *apud* Melo, 2008, p. 290).

In an attempt to widen the concept of communication beyond effects, it is important and fundamental to position communication studies so as to respond to questions that can be found on the agenda, according to the sociologist Craig Calhoun: "What features best describe the contemporary world?" Of the great changes that have occurred in the global landscape, which ones most fully define the present time? How can we shift from the perplexity that those great changes cause to an understanding within major interpretative frameworks? What is changing in the field of communication studies in terms of the analytical model with the change in the media landscape?"[2] These and other questions may help to strengthen the communication field in a more strategic, cohesive way to enrich

---

[2] See http://umaincertaantropologia.org/2014/08/13/o-papel-das-ciencias-sociais-em-um-mundo-em-mudanca-acelerada-fapesp/. Site accessed on 20 May 2015.

the division between scientific universalism and a humanistic focus, which has accompanied research in communication for a long time, through quantitative precision and depth of interpretation.

A media society: networks and being (the effects of reality)

Since the 1980s, a new concept has been present in the analytical landscape of media studies: mediatization. It arises in the dialogue with other concepts that have defined changes in society, becoming dominant in post-industrial society, post-modern society, and others. The concept reflects the fact that society has entered a new stage of hyper-mediatization that results from the emergence of multimedia, an explosion caused by hypertexts that many classify as globalization. "The interest of the concept of mediatization is that it makes it possible to consider as a whole several aspects of social change in industrialized societies that until now have been analysed and discussed in a relatively separate way" (Verón, 1997).

The concept of mediatization has seen controversy, like other, different concepts, although it can help with reflection thanks to its theoretical and empirical maturity (see Deacon & Stanyer, 2014 for a comprehensive overview). We know, however, that it needs to mature further as regards its empirical aspects so as to represent a reality in which the media are involved in different and important cultural, political and social endeavours. The concept of mediation, which is also involved in several controversies, operates and denotes regular communication processes that largely do not change in the relationships between the media, culture and society. Jesús Martín Barbero (2013) proposes three mediations that correspond to three aspects: sociability, rituality and technicity.[3] Based on this view, the two concepts – mediation and mediatization – are not mutually exclusive but instead complement one another; one highlights regular processes while the other focuses on transformational processes. The concept of mediatization places communication research within another historical framework.

---

[3] According to Barbero, "Sociality is related to social interaction, favouring individuals" negotiations with power and with institutions. Rituality is related to work routines and cultural production. Technicity refers to other practices of the production rationale through different languages in the field" (*apud* Ribeiro, 2013, p. 43).

Eliseo Verón (2014), in one of his last articles, proposed a mediatization theory from a semio-anthropological perspective. Its core point is the media phenomenon of making mental processes (cognitive processes) external, which goes beyond the "long historical sequence of media phenomena that are institutionalized in human societies, and their many consequences". He adds that the conceptual advantage of this perspective in the long term is to remind ourselves that what is happening in late modern societies began, in fact, a long time ago, since media phenomena "embody distortions and produce breaks in space-time".

> The initial stage of each crucial moment of mediatization can be dated, since it consists of a technical-communicational device that emerged and became stabilized in identifiable human communities, which means that it was adopted in one way or another. There is no implicit technological determinism here: at any time, appropriation of a technical device by the community may take one of many different forms; the formation of uses that eventually becomes institutionalized in one particular place and time around a communication device (a formation that may be properly called a medium) requires only historical explanation (Verón, 2014, p. 16).

Faced with such a large and broad-reaching challenge, studies on mediatization generally aim to engage in interdisciplinary research, connecting with other areas such as education, politics and religion so that each one brings its own contribution and effort to make a reflection.

> If it is correct that media have become more important to different fields of (late) modern society such as politics, education, religion and science, *scholars of media and communication research would do well to collaborate with* experienced experts in these fields: scholars of political science, pedagogy, religious studies, sociology of knowledge, etc. What we can bring to such an interdisciplinary dialogue is our experience as experts in researching processes of mediated communication (*mediation*) and their transforming potential (*mediatization*) (Hepp, Hjarvard & Lundby, 2015, p. 316).

From this interdisciplinary perspective, the concept of mediatization does not represent a social process of cause and effect, but instead a complex movement stimulated by the development of communication media and other dynamics that involve different institutions, in which the agents attempt to make use of the media for their own purposes and goals (*ibid.*). Mediatization, as an important concept in communication studies, calls attention to an issue that changes the concept of communication media in a reconciliation of interaction processes between social fields: they cease to be a "dependent variable", following functionalist theory, and go further than stating the central position of communication media, since the constitution and functioning of society – producing social semiosis – "are permeated by and crossed by presumptions and rationales of what I would call *the culture of the media*" (Fausto Neto, 2008, p. 92).

Mediatization in the processes of contemporary society is marked by two apparently contradictory processes that are highly present in the everyday lives of people and institutions: globalization and individualism. The social fields undergo the tensions of those two processes reached the economic area very early on, but it has also affected culture, religion, law, education, etc. However, in a world of confusing and uncontrollable changes, people tend to gather around primary identities. "In a world of global flows of wealth, power and images, the search for individual or collective identity, whether assigned or constructed, becomes the basic source of social significance." Later, Castells emphasizes the bipolar aspect of contemporary societies by saying "our societies are increasingly structured around the bipolar contrast of the Network and Being" (1999, p. 23).

Just as the concept of mediatization can be discussed from a semio-anthropological point of view, the concept of globalization can also be viewed from this perspective. Nayan Chanda, from India, has published a long text called *Bound Together*, which demonstrates that globalization emerged from, among other things, the "basic human need for a better and more rewarding life", which has been built over time by different actors, missionaries, adventurers and warriors. In this action, a link can be seen between the global and the individual: the search for a more enriching life, with the aim of accomplishing personal ambitions, abandoning or rebuilding natural habits, taking products, ideas and technology across borders through constant interrelations to create, according to Roland Robertson, "an intensification of the consciousness of the world as a whole" (Chanda, 2011, p. 20).

> "what the Greeks called oikumene" linking the fate of geographically separated communities, globalization, as a trend, has been with us since the beginning of history. The same forces, sometimes with different names, are at work today in connecting the world ever faster and more tightly. Multinational companies, non-governmental organizations, activists, migrants and tourists have been continuing the process of integration that began thousands of years ago (Chanda, 2011, p. 21).

In recent decades, a new economy has emerged in this long globalization process. Castells uses the words "information" and "global" to describe its fundamental, distinguishing aspects and to highlight its interconnections. It, "the economy", is an information economy because of the productivity and competitiveness of its agents, which basically depend on the ability to generate, process and apply effective forms of information. It is also global because the main production activities, circulation, consumption and other aspects involved are organized at global level. The economy is a "global" and "information" economy "because, under new historical conditions, productivity is generated and competition made in a global network of interaction" (Castells, 1999, p. 87).

A new society emerges, then, with a structural transformation observed in relationships of production, power and experience, i.e. a multidimensional transformation. The changes in the relationships mentioned above suggest a transformation in the material bases of social life, the concept of space and the concept of time.

> Networks are open structures capable of unlimited expansion, integrating new nodes as long as they can communicate within the network, in other words, as long as they share the same communication codes. A network-based social structure is an open and highly dynamic system that is open to innovation without threatening its balance. Networks are appropriate instruments for a capitalist economy based on decentralized innovation, globalization an concentration; for a policy designed for the instant processing of new public values

> and moods; and for a social organization that aims to replace space and invalidate time. But the morphology of the network is also a source of drastic reorganization of power relationships. The connections that link networks (for example, financial flows taking control of the media empires that influence political processes) represent those privileged with power... The convergence of social evolution and information technologies has created a new base material for performing activities throughout the social structure. That base material built in networks defines the dominant social processes, and therefore give form to the social structure itself (Castells, 1999, p. 499).

In light of these new bases for thinking about production, power and experience, it is possible to advance by attempting to describe Web 2.0, and exploring, above all, new access conditions and community appeals. The recent context became thought-provoking but misleading when a certain protagonism was sought in social networks to explain the reasons for mobilization in different parts of the world: the Arab Spring, demonstrations in the USA, in Spain, in Brazil, etc. In this complex context, created by the enthusiasm for technologies and the new connections in civil societies driven by "indignation and hope", many have sought explanations in new modes of information and communication technologies. The aim of the third and final part of this article is to demonstrate some characteristics of Web 2.0 to provide elements for a communication theory that is able to provide a framework for social changes and the implications of communication processes in social semiosis, i.e. the semiosis of mediatization.

Web 2.0: revolution of access and community appeals

This approach is concerned with showing the importance of the community, exercising citizenship on and over the internet, and its links with other institutions that are present in the public space. This perspective is part of a historical concern with considering communication media in conjunction with its implications for improving education, strengthening democracy, building citizenship, while being aware that the media will not replace schools, parliaments, and definitely not the many NGOs and other humanitarian bodies. Nonetheless, the internet is a space that includes, among other things, citizens' participation in a society that is more and more streamlined and framed within a world of business.

The internet, in its Web 2.0 stage, strengthens its own architecture in relation to communication media, which have been known since the creation of the press (radio, television, etc.). A single source (broadcaster) transmits a message and the silent masses receive it. Normally, telephones establish communication between two people. Until recently, most human activities were performed in small groups, but that was not technically viable. The internet enables communication between groups and their members and they broadcast information while making and remaking the groups, as has been seen in people's everyday lives over time.

It is important to highlight that the technology is incomplete, in transition, and there is a need to approach it in such a way as to safeguard "technical flexibility", since we can see that there is no determinism in the history of different techniques. A constructivist approach enables us to analyse a new technique and how it has developed in a landscape characterized by malleability. "There are always alternative routes to developing certain social forces and they determine which will be favoured and which will be ignored." It is possible to explain, therefore, through historical events and not through technical superiority "why, for example, we use refrigerators that run on electricity and not gas and why our cars run on petrol and not electricity" (Feenberg, 2014, p. 42).

It is from this perspective that Patrice Flichy (1995) was concerned with creating an innovation theory that seeks to characterize the different moments of a technique until it achieves a certain stability, which is not the case of the internet today. The author uses the second issue to discuss technical innovation: "How do social sciences pose the issue of innovation in the relationship between technique and use?" He proposes an approach that is based on the relationship between technique and use and studying individuals' social and technical actions.

> If it is acceptable to consider that technical objects are the result of three elements – actors' actions, chance, and social and technical limitations – research in social sciences can, therefore, have a dual function. On the one hand, it can help uncover the social and technical

> frameworks within which the action is located and, on the other hand, it can reveal the different cases of innovation in the past that form types of exercises regarding action for future innovators (Flichy, 1995, p. 234).

A technology, from this point of view, will be analysed as a constant confrontation/negotiation, through dynamic and relatively quick processes. "Based on the same technology, but using a slightly different design, it can serve the interests and needs of very different social groups" (Feenberg, 2014). This is also the point of view used here to consider the internet and its different networking models, which now coexist and represent possible formations that may dominate in the future: formations of consumption, information and community (*ibid.*) Since this article intends to consider elements for communication studies from a point of view that highlights social change, the community model will be emphasized.

The essence of the model in question is the chance for reciprocity, in which each participant moves between positions of broadcasting and receiving content through groups. They form types of online communities that have social and technical conditions and almost achieve the characteristics of face-to-face communities. The technical opportunity for reciprocity on the Internet carries a fundamental difference compared with traditional means of communication.

> The most original democratic implications of the internet have only just begun to emerge, and they have less to do with traditional politics than with new forms of agency that are on the way to redefining and broadening the political space. What we almost always identify as politics on the internet is simply an example of that wider phenomenon. To understand this new form of politics, we should again reconsider our way of thinking about the technique (Feenberg, 2014, p. 50).

Techniques are often considered based on their effectiveness, in the field of communications and in other scientific domains. However, the artefacts are political, which makes it possible to reconfigure the conditions of everyday life and influence the game of representing groups and communities in the public space. Representation is the main means of self-affirmation for communities in modern democracies and it is used by groups to defend their interests and values in the public space. By increasing visibility in societies it is possible to make speech and criticism more democratic. One issue arises in the new visibility methods: what happens when the boundaries that separate information and conversation are removed? A dual revolution occurs, according to Dominique Cardon:

> On the one hand, the right to speak in public is spreading throughout all of society; on the other, some private conversations are being incorporated into the public space. The public space extends to all people and in every direction... A very close relationship can be observed that unites them in the same process of the deepening and radicalization of contemporary individualism... The stagings of the self, of one's qualities and competences, are in step with a desire to broaden the area of visibility in which people show others their individuality in order have it recognized (Cardon, 2010, p. 11).

The Internet today stimulates all kinds of political thought, especially since action on social networks began to intensify, broadening the choices of conversation beyond information and consumption. The public space became wider, although with some changes as regards how it worked some time ago. Before the advent of Web 2.0, there was a divide between information and conversation. The public space was a place to exercise rationality, above all, and there was a clear boundary between information and intimate correspondence in the conversational sphere. The new wider public space can include operations known as "extimate" operations – a play on words that means externalizing the intimate. The space is then frequented more and more often by emotion, intimacy and passion in public discussions. As Patrice Flichy (2010) rightly said, in the digital age we are experiencing the rise of the amateur. The new public space is also occupied by the amateur, through the removal of boundaries between information and conversation.

The space described as "extimate" includes "a statement addressed to a limited number of receivers, who are known to a greater or lesser extent, through a device that can be accessed by all." Photography is one of the most widely used domains in this perspective of communication. Photos can be found that record gatherings of friends, meals, trips, tattoos, selfies, etc. Blogs are also spaces that reflect this new type of statement, and are often written even by renowned journalism professionals. There is a more personal touch to their blogs than their columns in printed newspapers or other media. Nevertheless, ordinary blogs, the result of the work of amateurs, are those that best reflect what is known as the "extimate" space, in which the construction of the self has become a technique for relating to others. In this public space, expression means engaging, through blog posts, comments, etc. (Flichy, 2010).

Most Internet collectives are the result of chance interactions, based around displaying identities, preferences, likes, etc. to form "weak cooperations". However, those "weak cooperations" may become strong and arm themselves with the resources and instruments of action, in a similar way to collectives in the real world, provided that there is an effort to mobilize online that is connected to methods of engaging individuals in the real world (Cardon, 2010).

In this perspective of debating, mostly without commands, there may be a shift from a notion of participatory democracy to cooperative democracy, built "from below" by a public that speaks without asking anybody. The democratization of the Internet is intimately linked to the many forms of visibility that the public space authorizes and enables. The forms of diversity made possible by the emergence of amateurs are still at an early stage, as are the features of cooperative democracy.

The communication field can certainly be enriched by and benefit from this productive and challenging time, helping to understand the changes in the internet and all of society as regards production, power and experience. Revisiting the background of the field and communication theories, understanding them better from the point of view of social theory, changes in context and strong trends, conditions for production and recognition of communication processes can all make for an exciting, stimulating journey through the world of the semiosis of mediatization based on a view of the field of communication studies.

Bibliography

Calhoun, C. (2011). Communication as social science (and more). *International Journal of Communication,* 5 (2011), pp. 1479–1496.

Cardon, D. (2010). *La démocratie internet – promesses et limites.* Paris: Éditions du Seuil.

Castells, M. (1999). *A sociedade em rede – a era da informação: economia, sociedade e cultura,* vol.1, São Paulo: Paz e Terra.

Chanda, N. (2011). *Sem fronteira.* Rio de Janeiro: Editora Record.

Deacon, D. & Stanyer, J. (2014). Mediatization: key concept or conceptual bandwagon? *Media, Culture and Society,* 36 (7), pp. 1032-1044.

Eco, U. (1978). *Apocalípticos e integrados.* São Paulo: Editora Perspectiva.

Fausto Neto, A. (2008). Fragmentos de uma "analítica" da midiatização. *Revista Matrizes,* 2, pp. 89-105.

Feenberg, A. (2014). Vers une théorie critique de l'internet. *Revue Tic & Société,* no. 1-2, vol. 8, pp. 29-56.

Ferreira, G. Marcus (2003). Em busca da disciplinarização da comunicação: da noção de campo aos domínios de pesquisa. In M. I. Vassalo de Lopes (ed.). *Epistemologia da comunicação* (pp. 253-276), São Paulo: Edições Loyola.

Flichy, P. (1995). *L´innovation technique – Récents développements en sciences sociales. Vers une nouvelle théorie de l´innovation.* Paris: Éditions de la Découverte.

Flichy, P. (2010). *Le sacre de l´amateur – sociologie des passions ordinaries à l´ère numérique.* Paris: Seuil.

Hepp, A., Hjarvard, S. & Lundby, K. (2015). Mediatization: theorizing the interplay between media, culture and society. *Media, Culture & Society,* no. 2, vol. 37, pp. 1-11.

Melo, J. Marques. (2008). La comunicación em la pedagogia de Paulo Freire. In A. Gumcio-Dragon & T. Tufte (eds.) *Antología de comunicación para el cambio social: leituras históricas y contemporâneas,* La Paz: Plural Editores.

Pooley, J. (2008). The new history of mass communication research. In D. Park & J. Pooley (eds.), *The history of media and communication research: contested memories* (pp. 43-69). New York: Peter Lang.

Proulx, S. (2010). Naissance du domaine des sciences de la communication dans le contexte militaire des années 1940 aux États-Unis. In *Racines oubliées dês sciences de la communication* (p. 40-41). Collection Les Essentiels d´Hèrmes, Paris: CNRS Éditions.

Ribeiro, L. C. & Tuzzo, S. A. (2013). Jesús Martín Barbero e seus estudos de mediação na telenovela. *Revista Comum & Inf,* no. 2, vol. 16, pp. 39-49.

Rogers, E. M. (1997). *A history of communication study – a biographical approach.* New York: The Free Press.

Schramm, W. (1997). *The beginnings of communication study in America: a memoir.* Thousand Oaks: Sage Publications. (edited by Steven H. Chaffee and Everret M. Rogers)

Sodré, M. (2012). Comunicação: caos criativo. *Revista Logos Comunicação & Universidade,* no. 37, Vol. 19, p. 6-16.

Varão, R. (2015). Uma guinada epistemológica: a utilização do termo comunicação a partir do Seminário Rockefeller, in *Anais do XIV Congresso Internacional IBERCOM.*

Varão, R. & Cunha, R. C. (2014). O conceito de comunicação em John Dewey, in *Anais II Congresso Mundial de Comunicação ibero-americana,* Universidade do Minho, Braga.

Verón, E. (1997). Esquema para el análisis de la mediatización. *Revista Diálogos de la Communicación*, no. 48, pp. 9-16.

Verón, E. (2013). *La semiosis social, 2 – ideas, momentos, interpretantes*. Buenos Aires: Paidós.

Verón, E. (2014). Teoria da midiatização: uma perspective semioantropológica e algumas de suas consequências. *Revista Matrizes*, no. 1, vol. 8, pp. 13-19.

Chapter 3

Descriptive indicators of photojournalistic treatment of political leaders from the standpoint of content analysis

Joaquín Lopez del Ramo

Introduction

Photography plays a fundamental role in building political actors' images. It is codified and transmitted through journalism channels, whether digital or print media. We cannot disregard the fact that the text-based message may occupy the central position of the informative discourse or, to be more precise, that the deep communicational core of the message may be found in the semantic symbiosis between text and image. However, it cannot be denied that, as Barthes (1992) argues, photographs carry a set of data (much of which is evaluative) that is codified and embodied autonomously, forming an independent structure, albeit a structure that complements the text (or vice-versa). This means that while it is not complex enough to "tell" the whole story, it is able to carry an independent and highly meaningful message.

This article intends to discuss the way in which information photography forms and represents the image of political leaders in day-to-day events or during election periods. Firstly, there is a description of the principles according to which photographs, as visual elements, form the base of their communicational power and their supposed value as a record of reality. The relationship between photography and political communication is then analysed, based on the fundamental conclusions of previous research. Finally, from the methodological viewpoint of content analysis, a coding sheet is proposed that includes descriptive indicators categorized by logical similarity. The sheet makes it possible to extract objective, relevant data on how political leaders are handled by photojournalism and, in accordance with that data, it is possible to understand how photography contributes to forming the journalistic message using its own codes.

Communication capacities of the image

Different semiotic systems also have different potentials for expression. In each case, they provide what we could call a specific "communication strength", and they do so in more or less favourable ways in order to transmit certain messages, depending on their nature, content and size. Compared to other types of language, visual language has a series of distinguishing features. Acaso (2009) describes them as follows:

- It is the oldest known communication system.
- It requires the least effort to read, and that is the reason for its great communication power. It is understood automatically to a great extent.
- It is the language that is most universal, and can be understood by a high proportion of different cultures.
- The signs in writing are always abstract, while images contain information that is similar to reality (isomorphism). It is what Barthes calls "the reality effect".

According to Peltzer (1991, p. 24), visual culture or visuality is to a certain extent the innate human ability to interpret and handle visual messages. We know how to read visual language without being taught, and we start to learn it as soon as we are born. It is largely the result of understanding through experience and repetition, although it is not formalized like writing. It is therefore common for people to only be able to read it and have knowledge that is superficial but enough to understand its major features. All these aspects are multiplied in the case of photography because it is the visual product that is most similar to the real thing it represents.

The photographer, like the designer in the graphics field, is the person who codifies the image using the technical and rhetoric resources of photographic language to create a representation of the real thing captured through the lens. As in any semiotic system, effectively performing the transmission process requires the receiver to have the ability to interpret or decode it. It is important to question whether or not an average media press reader has this ability, which we could call photographic literacy (as a specific variant of visual literacy), and gauge the level of such an ability. Given that an in-depth approach of the issue goes far beyond the limits of this study, it is assumed that today's general public has at least a basic level of photographic literacy. In any case, the interest here focuses on analysing what is transmitted by photographs and how it transmits information, i.e. what resources are used in the coding process.

Although there is a certain amount of controversy regarding the dominance of images or headlines in captivating readers' attention, especially in the digital press, several empirical research projects underline the pivotal communication power of images in journalism. Küpfer (1991) studied the visual paths and areas of attention on the pages of print newspapers and demonstrated two particularly significant aspects:

a) Articles with illustrations are read more frequently.

b) Images could be apprehended, understood and memorized much more quickly than text.

Coleman (2006, pp. 242-243) discusses the "picture superiority effect" and, based on work by Grimes (1990), Pezdeck (1977) and other researchers, she makes two categorical statements that follow the direction indicated above: "if the words and pictures are not congruent, people remember the information or perceive the viewpoint of the picture over the words" and "images exert a more powerful influence on memory and perceptions than text".

Muñiz, Igartua and Otero (2006), also referring to several authors, describe the cognitive and emotional effects of photographs in the press, and largely explain their communication power regardless of whether the medium used is print or digital:

- They reinforce the topic and bring additional data.
- They make the information visually more pleasant.
- They establish a certain worldview in the audience's mind and are more effective in doing so than the text itself.
- The effect of images remains over time and establishes memory. It is simpler to think in pictures.

To understand the impact of journalistic photography on the audience, there is another key factor: its credibility in the eyes of an average reader as an actual testament to a fact or situation (Sousa, 1998). Other researchers, such as Bruder (2007), lead to the same idea: for the public in general, photographs are considered to be reliable sources of information. Viewers are more liable to believe pictures that they see rather than what they hear or read. Alongside these reflections, Coleman (2006) underlines the importance of emotions caused by images and their effects on readers and viewers. She argues that in most cases receivers are not aware of this power, due to its apparent isomorphism with the real thing it shows, and so they are defenceless when they see it.

Although this idea appears to be deeply ingrained in the average audience, it is clear that, as Lorenzo Vilches (1995) highlights, it is a mirage or a cliché, because a photograph is a semblance or simulation of the truth rather than the truth itself. It is a representation of the truth as the result of coding performed by the photographer with a particular intent or connotative meaning that always involves a certain amount of manipulation. Lister (1997) argues that photographic discourse as a trustworthy reflection of reality has become clearly outdated and has been replaced by another that, from different perspectives, underlines its ideological and conventional character. The problem, again, is whether or not this is the case for the reader or whether it is so clearly and categorically the case.

Although the picture's "superiority effect" has been acknowledged, and although it is undeniably supported by real perception, there is consensus in noting that photographs alone are unable to articulate a full information report and, therefore, they need to be complemented by text. At the level of a particular news story, a multicode (strictly speaking, multimedia) plot is formed, in which each of the signs (in this case, visual and textual signs) carries its specific form to create a single message (the full "story"). The core meaning is equally shared between both types of sign, or rather, it turns towards one of them, depending on the communication and motivational force that they have. And there is no doubt that visual power gives photographs a certain advantage.

Political reporting and photography

Politics as a specialist area of journalism has historically had a prime position in reporting and has been widely accompanied by photographs, especially during election periods when, as Esteve and Fernández del Moral (1999) point out, the theme has its widest media coverage. Mazzoleni (2010) eloquently argues that current campaigns tend to be defined in journalistic and scientific language as "battles of image". The same author discusses a very important aspect: sections of the media are deliberately geared towards a certain (political) reality and give it characteristics that coincide with the worldviews (and political views) of each information company and journalist. This is so-called "bias", the implicit and inevitable distortion in the process of reproducing or "manufacturing" reality.

The way photojournalism handles politics and its leaders it not at all separate from this trend; on the contrary, it participates in it. As Koetsenruijter (2014, p. 1) points out: "The fact that a particular photograph appears in news media, can be seen as the result of collective rhetorical work done by spin doctors, photographers, journalists and editors". Besides ethical and professional considerations, this largely explains that photographs about politics and its leaders give the redundant and predictable impression of what Arterton (1978) mentioned when he spoke about political communication in general.

The examinations made in studies of photojournalism during electoral campaigns by Glassman and Kenney (1994), Roncero and Sampedro (1998), Waldman and Devitt (1998), del Valle (1999a), Chang, Wanta, Ryan and Lee (2004), Coleman and Wasike (2004) and López del Ramo (2008), among many others, demonstrate a series of coincidences that are widely found in descriptions of political photojournalism. They can be seen very distinctly and across the board, regardless of country, party or type of media. These features supported by the following points:

1. The pictures are very conventional, restricted to a few events, normally those that are most routine in election periods. Pictures of the "backstage" of politics, such as campaign team meetings or encounters between politicians and certain people or groups that (more or less discreetly) support them are published only very rarely.

2. In the photos of electoral process, candidates appear almost always as happy, dynamic, friendly and approachable people, and rarely appear worried or frustrated. At the same time, they play pre-established roles that form a type of mythic rhetoric, and have been labelled in different ways, according to Glassman and Kenney (1994, p. 6): “We also noted how often candidates were portrayed in one of the following seven roles: beloved leader, dynamic speaker, media star, the glad-to-see-you candidate, athlete/outdoorsman, father figure and family figure.”

3. In the way photographs in newspapers deal with different parties and leaders, clear, foreseeable ideological affinities can be seen, depending on economic interests, expectations of future support or editorial or ideological direction, providing legitimacy to politicians closer to them and removing it from those further away. Photographs can therefore become an instrumental element of electoral marketing transmitted by the media, although dressed as formal journalism.

4. The constant repetition of the same visual outlines by the press and television, year after year, election after election, has created stereotyped roles for politicians in the audience’s mind, during campaigns and in day-to-day activities, and they are established in the form of mental photographs. Eventually, through fatigue, they can weaken the credibility of politics and its main actors.

Focuses of the analysis and method

The approach to journalistic photography as an object of study suggests distinguishing between three possible levels of analysis:

a) The photograph itself, i.e. the content that appears within the image. Since it has independent meaning and possesses great potential for communication and expression, this is normally the only element considered in studies about photojournalism.

b) The text that accompanies the photograph, a contextual element that it is integrated with it in a news item or story with independent meaning that corresponds to or can be classified into a specific mode or genre of journalism: information, report, interview, etc. Studying the text-photo binomial involves a higher level of complexity, but it provides more complete knowledge of the message in its entirety. Normally, the focus is on the combined analysis of the headline and/or standfirst of the story and the image.

c) The general context in which the photograph is inserted; in the case of printed or digital press, this is the page. What is meant here is the location, design resources and layout that place a greater or lesser emphasis on the picture and therefore change the perception of it in the reader's eyes. The page on which it is published (front page, odd, even...), the size, or the position, for example, are factors which bring further meaning to the photograph and give it a certain amount of importance in the reader's eyes.

An analysis of how photojournalism deals with a subject is more complete the more it takes into account these three levels of analysis. Understanding the message overall requires taking into account the context into which the picture is inserted and involves the body providing the information. From our point of view, studying visual and written aspects is particularly important, since the photograph interacts with the text and therefore the two elements complement one another, enrich each other and provide each other with a new or wider meaning when they are studied together. This symbiotic message disappears or does not emerge if we detach or isolate them.

The interweaving between photograph and text gains particular significance in so-called Framing Theory, which is the equivalent of framing a news story. According to Entman (1993, pp. 52-53) "Framing essentially involves selection and salience. To frame is to select some aspects of a perceived reality and make them more salient in a communicating text, in such a way as to promote a particular problem definition, causal interpretation, moral evaluation, and/or treatment recommendation for the item described (...) Frames highlight some bits of information about an item that is the subject of a communication, thereby elevating them in salience. The Word salience itself needs to be defined: It means making a piece of information more noticeable, meaningful, or memorable to audiences."

Although Entman refers to text in particular, the framing process in written press media has a textual element and a visual element that are theoretically in agreement, in the sense that one supports and strengthens the other, i.e. both emphasize the same elements that define the framework established by the type of media regarding a specific matter or person. Therefore, it is important to discuss visual framing, which Coleman (*Ibidem*, p. 243) meticulously dissects, pointing out a central idea: "Examinations that include both visual and verbal framing of the same content in a single study are rare; however, such work is the best way to understand the holistic message that viewers receive". In summary, the North American professor is referring to an examination of the semantic integration between the photograph and the text that accompanies it as an essential strategy.

From a perspective that is more focused on the message of the photograph itself, it is important to note the presence of two points of analysis that may occur individually or together, depending on the interests and goals of the research:

- Analysis of the documentary features of the images, understood as a set of characteristics with denotative meaning that contain information. From those features, it is possible, for example, to quantify the photographic presence of the leaders or other figures, or the appearance of certain objects or elements of the scene recorded in the photograph.

- Analysis of the prevailing connotative-expressive features through which a specific vision of a person, party, institution, situation, event, etc. is transmitted. From this perspective, it is possible to trace and identify general and personal patterns, such as the creation of roles and topics. In any case, the connotative characteristics are those that, *a priori*, are more important to communication because they make up the underlying message transmitted by the photograph: how what is represented is represented.

Both forms of analysis focus on the content of images, so the most appropriate method is naturally content analysis, described by Igartua (2006) as a "research technique that makes it possible to discover the DNA of media messages (...) uncover their architecture, understand their structure, their basic components and how they work (...) to dissect any media communication product, to understand it from the inside, to know how it is made, to deduce and predict its influence mechanism". Content analysis has the added advantage of being based on the observation of reality and being supported by provable data, which can be used to make logical inferences.

Descriptors and application

The empirical studies mentioned above follow the methodological guidance of content analysis and use sheets or matrices formed of indicators. They work as descriptors of the photographic coding characteristics that are significant in each case. The number and diversity of variables considered in them are not excessive, and some are repeated particularly often, possibly because of their strong impact on the subjective load of the image. They are: angle, gestures, proximity and staging.

The matrix or sheet that has been created in this study comprises the three levels discussed above: the content of the photograph, the basic relationships between the image and the text and the context of the page. This is intended to provide a full analysis of photojournalism, i.e. an analysis that is not restricted to describing the characteristics of the photograph, but one that also describes the contextual elements around it that are liable to change the way in which it is understood by the reader. On the other hand, at strictly photographic level, the sheet takes into consideration a range of variables that form a wide, diverse repertoire, with the aim of recording significant and relevant connotative and denotative attributes regarding political leaders.

This analysis sheet is a specific variant of the "Analysis model for photojournalism from a documentary and information perspective" (López del Ramo, 2014), the design and formation of which were based on several earlier studies about press photography, especially those by Vilches (1995), Abreu (1993), Rodríguez Merchán (1993), Alonso Erausquin (1995), Sousa (1998 y 2004), del Valle (1999a and 1999b) and Marzal (2004), as well as the coding books drawn up by the author (López del Ramo, 2010). It is designed to be a model open to the inclusion of other indicators and values and to modification of those currently in it.

In keeping with the considerations above, the sheet is based around two general categories which group indicators together by logical similarity: the attributes of the photograph (characteristics that are visible and can be analysed within the frame of the image) and attributes relating to how it is placed on the page (features of contextual elements: layout and text). In turn, both categories are subdivided into several groups to form the following structure:

Photograph attributes

1. Biographical-documentary data
2. Photographic coding indicators
    (a) Area captured
    (b) Focus and movement
    (c) Layout
    (d) Gestures
    (e) Light and colour

Contextual characteristics

3. Location
4. Layout
5. Relationship between text and image

The indicators are listed below and classified, with a brief description and the values that can be inserted:

Photograph attributes

Indicator and description	Values
1.1. Protagonist(s)	Identification. Determined by proximity and/or focus
1.2. Role Function(s) of the main and/or secondary protagonist	Identification
1.3. Party Political party to which he/she belongs	Identification
1.4.Other (animate or inanimate) actants	Identification
1.5. Existence of symbolic items	Identification
1.6. Scenography Surroundings, elements in the surrounding area, clothes	Identification and brief description
1.7. Episode Framework surrounding the specific episode to which the image belongs	Identification
1.8. Date on which image was taken	Identification

Table 3.1: Biographical-documentary data

2.1. Area captured	
Indicator and description	**Values**
2.1.1. Framing Field of vision captured	General, group, close up
2.1.2. Angle Use of perspective distortion	Neutral, telephoto, wide-angle, fisheye
2.1.3. Vertical tilt Position of the image captured on the vertical axis	Neutral, low-angle, high-angle
2.1.4. Horizontal panning	Move to the left, move to the right
2.2. Focus and movement	
Indicator and description	**Values**
2.2.1. Type of focus Level of focus	Total, selective, unfocused

2.2.2. Amount of momentum Predominant or visible momentum of the main figure	Static, moderate action, rapid action
2.2.3. Capturing movement Way of capturing moving objects in the image	Frozen, moving, sweeping
2.3. Composition	
Indicator and description	**Values**
2.3.1. Balance Level of symmetry	Formal, informal, imbalance
2.3.2. Position of the protagonist in the photo Use of attraction points (third parties)	Centred, left, right
2.3.3. Interposed objects Presence of interposed objects in the foreground	Identification
2.3.4. Overlapping and superposition Presence of overlapping or superimposed elements with the figure or any part of the figure	Identification
2.3.3. Lateral position of protagonist Side of the body captured	Frontal, slanted, right side, left side, behind
2.4. Gestures	
Indicator and description	**Values**
2.4.1.Do actors have the same gestures? Contrast between the figures in the photo	Yes, no
2.4.2. Facial expression Of the main protagonist	List of values to be specified
2.4.3. Direction of gaze Of the main protagonist towards the shot	Frontal, right side, left side, above, below
2.4.4. Position of hands Of the main protagonist	Description
2.4.5. Stance Of the main protagonist	Normal, expansive, contractive
2.4.6. Proxemics Perceived distance between protagonist and the other figures in the image	Intimacy, personal space, social space, public space

2.4.7. Body contact Between the main protagonist and any of the figures around him/her	Intense-intimate, medium-affectionate, touching, no contact
2.4.8. Is it a portrait?	Image produced by figures posing
2.5 Light and colour	
Indicator and description	**Values**
2.5.1. General light contrast Level of difference between light and dark	Balanced, high, low
2.5.2. Spread of light Regarding the image as a whole	Balanced, diffuse, harsh
2.5.3. Direction of light Regarding the main protagonist	Direct, from the side, from above, from below
2.5.4. Colour Type of colour use	Black and white, colour, some areas coloured
2.5.5. Dominant colours Clear change in all natural colouring	Indicate tone

Table 3.2: Photographic coding indicators

Contextual characteristics

3.3. Location	
Indicator and description	**Values**
3.1. Page	Front page, even-numbered page, odd-numbered page, back page
3.1. Section	Identification
3.1. Informative style of text	Information, interpretation, opinion
4.Layout	
Indicator and description	**Values**
4.1. Size Measured in columns and % of height or in modules	Specification of a numerical value
4.2. Location on page	Upper, centre, lower
4.3. Colour Type of colour use	Black and white, colour, some areas coloured

4.4. Style of outline Graphic outline of the image	Regular, irregular, cut-out
4.5. Caption	Specify whether used or not
5. Relationship between text and image	
Indicator and description	**Values**
5.1. Communication function Contribution of information by the photograph regarding the text of the news piece	Informative: offers data not included in the text Reiterative: repeats data from the text but adds no new data Decorative: carries irrelevant data
5.2. Correspondence between the news story and the photo Agreement between the central topic of the news story and the photograph. Does not include archive photos, since they do not match the story they illustrate	Yes, no, tangentially

Table 3.3: Photographic coding indicators

Conclusions

1. Photographs are elements that carry a communicational message that has a great power of attraction and expressiveness, and they establish perception, which creates "mental frameworks" in the receiver; alone, however, they are not able to tell a full story, notwithstanding some exceptional situations.

2. Photographs reproduce reality and do so credibly in the eyes of most readers, although they are in fact subjective. They are, to a greater or lesser extent, a manipulated version of reality and the result of a deliberate journalistic or editorial strategy. Analysing the coding characteristics of reality through photographs is extremely useful in the scope of communication, particularly in the political area.

3. Stereotypes, routine conventionalism and ideological bias prevail in how the media deals with politics and political figures in its photographs, above all during electoral campaigns. An excess or abuse of "clichés" and excessive predictability may explain the distance between the public and politicians, by broadcasting the impression of a prefabricated image, hollow rhetoric or even falseness.

4. Research on political photojournalism has a particularly diverse and enriching field of application: documentary research, visual framing, description of patterns, roles and stereotypes of leaders, textual and visual analysis, etc. In turn, these perspectives can be combined with others, such as the story, theme, type of media, or comparative studies of some or all of these factors.

5. Within the methodological technique of content analysis, appropriately determining the characteristics of the photojournalistic message demands the use of coding sheets composed of the indicators that most completely and faithfully provide objective data on the internal meaning of the photograph, but also data on the contextual elements that frame and accompany it.

6. The analysis sheet presented in this study is intended to be a useful tool for structured, complete and systematic coding, and it is hoped that it can be used to obtain in-depth, exhaustive relevant data on how photojournalism deals with political leaders.

Bibliography

Acaso, M. (2009). *El lenguaje visual.* Barcelona: Paidós Iberica.

Abreu, C. (1993). *La fotografía periodística: una aproximación teórico-práctica.* Tenerife: Ediciones Universidad de La Laguna.

Artenton, F. C. (1978). Las organizaciones de la campaña enfrentan el entorno de los medios. In D. Graber (ed.), *El poder de los medios en la política.* Argentina: Grupo Editor Latinoamericano.

Alonso Erausquin, M. (1995). *Fotoperiodismo: formas y códigos.* Madrid: Síntesis.

Barthes, R. (1992). *Lo obvio y lo obtuso. Imágenes, gestos, voces.* Barcelona: Paidós.

Bruder, K. (2007). The effects of news photographs on a reader's retention. COM 350. Available at: `http://www.katebruder.com/Writing_&_Design_files/Photographs%20and%20Information%20Retention.pdf` [Retrieved: 21/08/2014].

Chang, K.; Wanta, W.; Ryan, E. & Lee, T. (2004). Looking Presidential: a Comparison of Newspaper Photographs of Candidates in the United States and Taiwan. *Asian Journal of Communication*, 14 (2), 121-139.

Coleman, R. (2006). Framing the pictures in our heads. Exploring the framing and agenda-setting effects of visual images. In P. D'angelo & J. Kuypers (eds.), *Doing news framing analysis: empirical, theoretical, and normative perspectives* (pp. 233-261). New York: Routledge.

Coleman, R.; Wasike, B. (2004). Visual elements in public journalism newspapers in an election: a content analysis of the photographs and graphics in campaign 2000. *Journal of Communication*, 54 (3), 456-473.

Entman, R.M. (1993). Framing: toward classification of a fractured paradigm. *Journal of communication*, 43 (4), 1-8.

Esteve Ramirez, F. & Fernández del Moral, J. (1999). *Áreas de especialización Periodística.* Madrid: Fragua.

Glassman, C. & Kenney, K. (1994). Mythe and presidential campaign photographs. *Visual Communication Quarterly*, 1 (4), 4–7.

Grimes, T. (1990). Encoding TV news messages into memory. *Journalism Quarterly*, 67, 757-766.

Igartua, J.J.(2007). *Métodos cuantitativos de investigación en comunicación.* Barcelona: Bosch.

Koetsenruijter, W. (2014). Visual rhetoric or the rhetoric of power in images of world leaders. A model for measuring social distance in news portraits of world leaders. *Electornic Scientific Journal*, 12. Available at: `http://rhetoric.bg/` [Retrieved: 18/08/2014]

Küpfer, N. (1991). Esa caprichosa Mirada. *Revista de la Universidad Católica de Chile*, vol. 7, 109-120.

Lister, M. (1997). *La imagen fotográfica en la cultura digital.* Barcelona: Paidós.

López del Ramo, J. (2008). Imagen fotoperiodística de los líderes políticos en campaña electoral: encuadre, escenografía y gestualidad. *Ibersid: revista de sistemas de información y documentación*, vol. 2, 177-183.

López del Ramo, J. (2014). Modelo de análisis de contenido de la fotografía periodística desde el plano documental e informativo. *Registro de la Propiedad Intelectual como obra científica.* Número M-001449/2014.

Marzal Felici, J. (2004). Metodología de análisis de la fotografía Web www.analisisfotografía,uji.es (Online). Available at: `http://www.analisisfotografia.uji.es/root2/METODOLOGIA%20ANALISIS%20FOTO%2023-11-2007.pdf` [Retrieved: 22/09/2014].

Mazzoleni, G.P. (2010). *La comunicación política.* Madrid: Alianza Editorial.

Muñiz, C.; Igartua, J. J.; Otero, J. A. (2006). Imágenes de la inmigración através de la fotografía de prensa: un estudio de los principales periódicos españoles. *Comunicación y Sociedad,* 19 (1), 103-128.

Lister, M.(1997). *La imagen fotográfica en la cultura digital.* Barcelona: Paidós.

Peltzer, G. (1991). *Periodismo iconográfico.* Madrid: Ediciones Rialp.

Pezdek, K. (1977). Cross-modality semantic integration of sentence and picture memory. *Journal of Experimental Psychology,* vol. 3, 515-524.

Rodriguez Merchán, E.(1993). *La realidad fragmentada.* Madrid: Universidad Complutense.

Roncero Villa, T. & Sampedro Blanco, V. (1998). ¿Noticias o carteles electorales? Imagen política en prensa e infopropaganda. *Revista Latina de Comunicación Social* 10. Available at: `http://www.ull.es/publicaciones/latina/a/22salamanca/22sala.htm` [Retrieved: 19/09/2014].

Sousa, J.P. (1998). *Fotojornalismo preformativo.* Porto: Edições Universidade Fernando Pessoa.

Sousa, J. P. (2004). *Fotojornalismo. Introdução à história, às técnicas e à linguagem da fotografia na imprensa.* Florianópolis-SC: Letras Contemporâneas.

Valle Gastamiza, F. del (1999a). El análisis documental de la fotografía. In F. del Valle Gastaminza (ed.), *Manual de Documentación Fotográfica.* Madrid: Síntesis.

Valle Gastamiza, F. del (1999b). Lenguaje fotográfico y fotografía Política en el diario El País. *Actas del Congreso Internacional La Lengua y los medios de comunicación.* vol. 1 (pp. 467-473). Madrid: Universidad Complutense.

Vilches, L. (1987). *Teoría de la imagen periodística.* Barcelona: Paidós (1ª ed.)

Vilches, L. (1995). *La lectura de la imagen.* Barcelona: Paidós (2ª ed.)

Waldman, P. & Devitt, J. (1998). Newspaper photographs and the 1996 presidential election: the question of Bias. *Journalism and Mass Communication Quarterly,* 75, 302-311.

Chapter 4

The emergence of Spain's *Podemos* (We Can) Party: Challenges for political communication practice and study

Karen Sanders

Introduction[1]

In the May 2014 European Parliament elections, *Podemos* [We Can], a political party registered in March 2014, won five seats and 1.2 million votes. By October 2014, 14% of Spaniards said they would vote for *Podemos* in the next general elections and by January 2015 this figure had risen to 23.9%, pushing *Podemos* into second place after the governing conservative Partido Popular (People's Party or PP), for whom 27.3% of Spaniards declared their intention to vote, leaving the Partido Socialista Obrero Español (Spanish Worker Socialist Party or PSOE) in third position with 22.2% (Centro de Investigaciones Sociológicas or CIS, 2015, January). When asked "Supposing general elections were held tomorrow, what party would you vote for?" *Podemos* was placed first with 19.3% voters declaring their support, followed by PP (12.9%) and PSOE (12.4%) (CIS, 2015, January). It may be the case that these polling figures represented the high-water mark of nationwide support for *Podemos*,[2] nevertheless many commentators declared that these survey figures signalled the end of the duopoly that had dominated Spanish politics in the democratic era (Cué, 2015, February 4). This chapter charts

[1] The author acknowledges and thanks Rosa Berganza and Roberto de Miguel for their contribution to the research relating to *Podemos* as a populist party. This research has been undertaken for a forthcoming publication coordinated by the COST Action IS1308 on populist political communication.

[2] The CIS survey of April 2015 placed *Podemos* in third place after PP and PSOE with 15.5% of the intended vote.

the emergence of *Podemos* on the European scene, its relationship to populist politics and examines what challenges it poses for the practice and study of political communication.

The *indignados* and the decline of trust in politics

Since Spain's democratic transition between 1975 and 1982 after 36 years of General Franco's dictatorship, the political landscape has been dominated by the centre-right PP and the centre-left PSOE. From victory in the traumatic 2004 elections, marked by the tragic Madrid train bombings in which 191 people died, the Socialist Party was in power until its defeat in the 2011 elections by PP. The conservatives proceeded to pursue with greater vigour the austerity policies initiated by the Socialists in the context of an unemployment rate of 23% in 2011 and youth unemployment which had surpassed 50% by 2012 (Historical Forex Data, March 2015).

In May 2011, a movement known as the *indignados* ("the outraged") began a series of protest meetings centred on Madrid's Puerta del Sol, calling for more participatory politics, the end of austerity policies and of "PPSOE" dominance of public life to allow the development of citizen politics in Spain (Alcaide, 2011, May 17). Adept social media users, the movement's organizers spread the messages of the *indignados* through Twitter hashtags and other social media and succeeded in galvanizing a significant cross-section of Spanish society. In the words of one of the movement's activists: "The parties have become large, inefficient and enormously corrupt companies and citizens are aware of this and have said to them: 'You don't represent us?' " (cited in Alcaide, 2011, May 17).

Lack of trust in mainstream Spanish politics and politicians was a prevailing theme of the *indignados*' protests. According to survey figures produced by Spain's Centre for Sociological Research (CIS, 2015), political trust in Spanish mainstream parties has steadily declined from a peak of over 60% in 2004 to little over 30% by 2015. Politicians and political parties were also consistently at the bottom of the list of those institutions receiving citizens' approval, scoring only nine and ten per cent respectively (Metroscopia cited in Toharia, 2013, January 10). Spaniards were not only disenchanted with their national politicians. The European Commission's Eurobarometer (2014) revealed that the years of crisis beginning in 2008 had eaten into the Spanish people's trust in European Union (EU) institutions and the EU itself: trusted by over 50% of the Spanish in 2004, this figure had fallen to 31% by September 2013. Declining rates of trust in mainstream western politics and politicians are a consistent finding of diverse survey data (see, for example, Edelman Trust Barometer, 2014) and have provided a window of opportunity for the development of populist parties, particularly of the radical right (see Bale, 2012).

Falling levels of institutional trust are in and of themselves not necessarily negative for democracies but there is evidence to suggest that democracies cannot do without trust altogether (see Warren, 1999). For example, in societies where citizens do not trust those who govern them to make honest use of money collected through taxes, citizens are likely to be less inclined to pay taxes and, indeed, find ways of avoiding payment of them. In complex societies, trust allows complexity to be reduced; however, in democracies it also implies relinquishing "the opportunity to influence decision-making, on the assumption that there are shared or convergent interests between truster and trustee" (Warren, 1999, p.4).

Some thinkers consider institutional political trust to be unimportant for the stability of democracies as compared to the role of interpersonal trust and subjective well-being (Inglehart, 1999). While the complex question of the relationship of political trust to flourishing democracies is beyond the scope of this chapter, discontent with mainstream parties and politicians is a feature of contemporary European politics that appears to provide an opportunity for the emergence of non-mainstream political parties as can be seen in Greece with the rise of Syriza, Le Front National in France and *Podemos* in Spain. Often referred to as "populist" by media commentators, these parties do not generally have the tarnished reputational legacies of the mainstream parties (although this quickly changes when they achieve power) and can offer citizens a fresh opportunity for trust.

Populist politics in Spain

Populism is a highly contested political concept (Jagers and Walgrave, 2007, p.321). In the European context it has been usually associated with the rise of radical right parties such as Le Pen's Front National in France and the Flemish Block in Belgium (see Mudde,

2007). In Latin America, however, populism has been associated with the development of left-wing political movements, led by charismatic politicians such as Venezuela's Hugo Chavez and Peru's Alberto Fujimori, who employ a Manichean discourse of "us/them", "people/elite", positioning themselves as "outsiders" who reject traditional political structures (see Rivas and Araque, 2011). In an effort to provide some conceptual order to what we understand by populism, Jagers and Walgrave (2007) developed a typology that can encompass both left and right-wing populist politics and depends on an understanding of populism as a political communication style. They propose a thin definition of populism "as a political communication style of political actors that refers to the people" (2007, p.322). A thick definition of populism contains two further elements, namely the expression of anti-elite feelings and the promotion of the idea that the people are a monolithic, homogenous group positioned against other categories (ethnic or religious groups, for example) who should be excluded (2007, p. 322). The typology is fourfold: *complete populism* characterized by reference and appeals to the people, anti-elitism and exclusion of outgroups; *excluding populism* defined by reference and appeals to the people and exclusion of outgroups; *anti-elitist populism* which includes reference and appeals to the people and anti-elitism and, finally, *empty populism* defined by reference and appeals to the people.

As we have seen, *Podemos* emerged from Spain's 2011 *indignados* movement and while its activists and leaders claim that it is "neither of the left nor of the right" (Carlin, 2015, January 21), most commentators disagree, considering it to be a left-wing, populist party (see Carlin, 2015, January 21; Muñoz, 2015, February 1). The party was founded when Spain continued to suffer the effects of a severe recession that produced some of the highest unemployment rates in the European Union. While ordinary Spaniards endured considerable hardship, they were dismayed to see that members of the Spanish business and political establishment (including the king's son-in-law, board members of savings banks and national and regional politicians) had indulged in venal practices of self-enrichment that fed public dissatisfaction with the political system. The system itself also appeared to be on the point of breakdown with the growth of Catalonian demands for independence, enhancing the sense of crisis felt by ordinary people. It is in this context that *Podemos* made its appearance, using a rhetoric typically associated with populism, as we shall see below, in which the party positioned itself against the ruling "political class" who sought to defend their own narrow interests against those of the people (Errejón, 2014; Stobart, 2014).

Casals (2013), however, argues that this is not the first time that populist politics has existed in Spain. He considers *Podemos*' rise to be part of a third wave of populist politics beginning with the 2008 economic recession and having much in common with other European populist movements such as Italy's Beppe Grillo Five Star movement and Greek's Syriza Party, who all share an anti-elitist discourse reflecting public resentment at austerity measures and a rejection of and alienation from mainstream politics. Casals includes new parties such as Unión Progreso y Democracia and Equo in this third wave of populist politics. He suggests that there have been two previous waves of populist politics: a first wave (1989-2000) characterized by what he considers to be an Italianization of Spanish politics understood as the entry into politics of charismatic individual businessmen and lawyers such as the judge, Balthasár Garzón and businessman, Jesús Gil; he distinguishes a second wave (2001-2008) characterized by the emergence of new political parties such as the extreme right-wing Plataforma per Catalunya (PxC) and parties such as Solidaritat Catalana per la Independência (SI) and Candidatura d'Unitat Popular (CUP), all founded in Catalonia and sharing the exclusionary politics of Italy's Liga Norte or France's Front National.

Casals' chronology of Spanish populist politics attributes the emergence of populist actors and parties to particular economic and social contexts. He does not, however, provide a conceptualization of populist politics which would allow us to test the suitability of the populist label ascribed to the diverse political actors which he describes as populist. In addition, the term "populist" as used by Spanish commentators is understood exclusively in a pejorative manner when applied either to left or right-wing parties and/or politicians. For this reason, Jagers and Walgraves' (2007) typology of populism with reference to a style of political communication is useful. It allows us to examine the characteristics of political actors in accordance with a parsimonious, non-evaluative definition of populism.

As we have seen, Spain's deepening recession between 2008 and 2013 brought demands for democratic reforms that would create a more participatory democracy, replacing the existing model of representative democracy that was perceived to have failed the people. Movements such as the 15-M movement embodied these demands and led protests against the tide of corruption that seemed to be engulfing Spanish politics. "The people against the Parliament" became the slogan of these movements, expressing the view that mainstream politics were broken and no longer represented the citizens' interests.

Whereas in many European countries, populist radical right (PRR) parties were the mouthpiece for the politics of disillusion and protest (see Mudde, 2007), in Spain radical right parties have achieved no widespread electoral support. As Alonso and Kaltwasser (2015, p.3) point out, "there are only two countries in which PRR parties have *never* obtained more than one per cent of the vote in any national election: Portugal and Spain".

Reframing Spanish politics

In its short existence, *Podemos* has sought to reframe Spanish politics with a well-thought out communication strategy and style built around four principal messages which the key actors have explained in numerous media interviews and public presentations (see, for example, Bescansa, 2014, July 18). The declarations and actions of the leaders of *Podemos* provide evidence for this well-crafted and professional communication strategy that makes clever use of a combination of mainstream and social media (see Carlin, 2015, January 29, for example). It is also clear that the formulation of their strategy and its content has drawn on their own professional expertise as academics trained in political science who have studied the field of public opinion and the uses of political communication.

Gaining visibility and generating conversation

Examining first *Podemos*' communication strategy, it can be characterized as using a combination of mainstream and social media to engage the public. Before the party's foundation, Pablo Iglesias had already gained considerable television experience through his political debate programme *La Tuerka*, which first appeared in November 2010 on the television channel Tele K and then later on Canal 33. Iglesias himself defined the project as: "An attempt at experimenting in political communication" in which he would use a format "that normally would have been the exclusive heritage of the enemy ... to normalize a series of reasonings that, at first, were removed from the mainstream" (cited in Machuca, 2014, February 2). Having gained media experience and increased visibility, Iglesias was invited to participate in the right-wing political debate show "El Gato al Agua" of Intereconomía, a highly conservative television channel where Iglesias appeared for the first time in April 2013. His opening words were: "It is a pleasure to cross the enemy's lines and to chat with [people from] the Comanche territory" (cited in Machuca, 2014, May 27). His appearance led to invitations to high visibility mainstream shows on *La Sexta* and *Cuatro*, national channels widely watched across Spain. *Podemos* but more particularly Pablo Iglesias began to build a strong public presence and visual and rhetorical style characterised by informality and a straightforward conversational style.

Podemos also effectively engaged the public through the use of social media such as Twitter and Facebook as well as the employment of apps and software such as Loomio and Agora to facilitate collaborative and participatory work on building *Podemos*' electoral programme (Carlin, 2015, January 21). Their use of social media for the 2014 European elections made clear the generational gulf between the younger leaders of *Podemos* and those of the mainstream parties led by men and women at least one generation older. Iglesias opened a Twitter account in 2010 and habitually used it to communicate with his followers. By the time of the European elections he had around 500,000 followers (see figure 4.1 and Bollero, 2014, August 16). The PP candidate, Miguel Arias Cañete, only created his Twitter account shortly before the European elections and he used it exclusively to send messages to his almost 20,000 followers having no interaction with them whatsoever (see Rodríguez, 2014, May 25).

On Facebook and YouTube, *Podemos* also outdid its mainstream rivals in terms of presence and content. By August 2014, the party had around 700,000 Facebook likes compared to PP's and PSOE's less than 200,000 and *Podemos* had triple the numbers of subscribers to its YouTube videos, registering over 30,000 compared to PSOE's less than 10,000 and PP's less than 5,000 (see Bollero, 2014, August 16). *Podemos*' digital natives used social media as means to generate a conversation with sections of the Spanish population who had not previously voted. A post-electoral study showed that *Podemos* won many votes from those who had abstained in the previous elections or those who were voting for the first time (see Institut Balear de Estudios Sociales, 2014, June 1). This young demographic (18-21) made up part of the 29% of *Podemos*' electorate who were aged between 18 and 35.

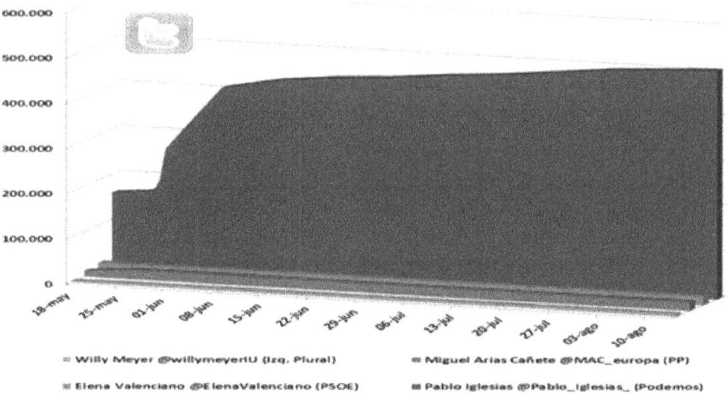

Figure 4.1: Source: Twitter Count 2014 cited in http://www.3djuegos.com/comunidad-foros/tema/32214216/0/podemos-se-consolida-como-la-primera-fuerza-politica- en-redes-sociales/

Changing the terms of the conversation

Examining next *Podemos*' key messages, the point of departure is their positioning as "the people" in contrast to the political and business elites who govern for themselves rather than for the country and to whom *Podemos*' leaders refer constantly as the "*casta*" (political caste). *Podemos*' positioning of itself as "the people" is aesthetically expressed in both the sartorial and rhetorical style of its leaders. In contrast to the principally formal dress style of politicians from the two mainstream parties, Pablo Iglesias and his companions dress informally and speak in simple, direct language. However, it should be noted that on 26 July 2014 PSOE elected the young, photogenic Pedro Sánchez as its leader who has adopted a more informal style in speech and dress similar to that of Pablo Iglesias. The second key message linked to the first is the emphasis placed on the corruption of mainstream Spanish politics exemplified by the constant stream of scandals affecting both mainstream parties and the phenomenon of "revolving doors" where members of previous and current governments pass seamlessly from their government roles to well-paid positions on state and private corporate boards (Errejón, 2011). Elite corruption is contrasted with *Podemos*' principled approach to politics, expressed, for example, in their renunciation of the full European Parliamentary salary (Fariza, 2014, July 2). In third place, *Podemos*' style of doing politics, exemplified by their use of "*círculos*" or circles that develop policy ideas using online participatory software, expresses their message that they stand for a new participatory politics that will replace the unrepresentative politics of the elite. In Iglesias' own words: "They are open to everybody, they are spaces of popular protagonism and they have to have their own journey in terms of what they want to propose. We don't want them to be spaces in which we give the orders but instruments for the self-organization of the people." Finally, the leaders of *Podemos* have refused to accept what they proclaim to be the false dichotomies of left and right. Their message is that they offer "common sense" politics. According to Íñigo Errejón, the chief campaign strategist of *Podemos*: "Left and right are metaphors, they are names and nothing else and they are not eternal. We represent common sense in a transversal, popular identity against the oligarchy" (cited in Carlin, 2015, January 29). A post-electoral study of the 2014 European Parliament elections (Institut Balear de Estudios Sociales, 2014, June 1) showed that *Podemos* picked up a large number of votes from the two main left-wing parties with the Socialists (PSOE) losing most voters, closely followed by Izquierda Unida. A small number of votes were gained from the ruling conservative party, PP.

This preliminary analysis of *Podemos*' communication approach shows that it appears to conform to the definition offered by Jagers and Walgrave (2007) of an anti-elitist populist party: its leaders make frequent references and appeals to the people, use anti-establishment rhetoric and call for wider inclusion. They do not, as radical right groups do, define outgroups that should be excluded. However, it should be emphasized that this categorization must be treated with caution until more systematic research can be carried out to provide a rigorous analysis of *Podemos*' political communication.

Normalizing *Podemos*

After the euphoria of the 2014 European Parliamentary results and subsequent polls placing *Podemos* in first or second place in voting intention in early 2015, there are signs that the *Podemos* phenomenon is beginning to lose some of its lustre. The party and its leaders have experienced unrelenting media scrutiny and opposition attack that has sought to undermine its key messages. For example, much has been made of the fact that party leaders have had financial and ideological connections to the Venezuelan government with the implicit suggestion that *Podemos* shares Chavism's populist authoritarian approach to politics and is not as pure as it pretends. This last accusation is particularly damaging for a party which has positioned itself as the pure anti-corruption party of the people. Accusations of corruption (see Gaceta.es, 2014, December 4) have been pursued against two key *Podemos* figures: Íñigo Errejón for breaching his university contract and Juan Carlos Monedero for a delay in paying taxes on income earned advising Latin American left-wing governments. Monedero's declarations in April 2015 that *Podemos* was falling into the same errors as its rivals were seized on by critical media and politicians as showing that *Podemos* was just as inauthentic as the parties it attacks. His subsequent resignation was framed as *Podemos*' first major crisis (Manetto, 2015, April 30).

Results in regional elections in March 2015 saw PSOE maintaining its 37-year hold on power in Andalucia with 35% of the vote, PP second with almost 27% and *Podemos* in third place with 15%. These elections also saw the emergence of another political grouping onto the national stage, Ciudadanos [Citizens], the Spanish reincarnation of the Catalonian Ciutadans party, which won 9% of the vote and, despite its own rejection of ideological labels, was seen by voters and commentators as a "*Podemos* of the right" (see Escolar, 2015, January 15).

Challenges for political communication research and practice

The rise of *Podemos* is a key development for Spanish politics but also, I will argue now, suggests some interesting challenges for political communication research and practice. The emergence of *Podemos* and other political groups together with the popular distrust of mainstream politicians and political parties has placed the phenomenon of political populism firmly on the Spanish political and public agenda. This is, however, an underexplored area of research and to date there is no systematic analysis of populist communication in Spain with regard to actors, media and citizens. Second, much scholarly analysis of political communication and, in particular, electoral communication poses what one could describe as a false dichotomy where professional campaigns are considered as producing bystander democracies (see, for example, Negrine 2007). Professional communication is seen as somehow incompatible with democratic communication that empowers the citizen. However, *Podemos*' highly professional approach to political communication, using to great effect both traditional and social media, has at the same time sought to democratize this communication. In other words, in research and practice it may be possible to consider "good" political communication as not only being about effective campaigns because political actors "win" but also about being "good" from the perspective of the democratic and/or civic values they promote (see Sanders and Canel, 2013; Scammell, 2013). This could help us to think about political communication practice and research that defines and operationalizes these values. Do campaigns, for example, increase political knowledge and efficacy? To what extent do political actors encourage and facilitate participation? How responsive and accountable are they to citizens? In other words, what are the democratic or civic dimensions that we can seek to embed in all political communication?

Third, and finally, the rise of *Podemos* places the idea of the presentation of authenticity at the centre of its politics. Authenticity is a complex concept. It involves the quality of realness, of something being genuine and not an imitation and, for human beings, the idea of being true to oneself. When we believe something or someone to be authentic we are more likely to trust them. A major challenge for many politicians is to overcome the citizens' sense that they are inauthentic, that they simply parrot party lines to win votes and elections. Understanding the construction of authenticity, how it is achieved or undermined in different media environments also provide interesting challenges for future political communication research and practice.

Bibliography

Alcaide, S. (2011, May 17). Movimiento 15-M: los ciudadanos exigen reconstruir la política. *El País.* Retrieved from http://politica.elpais.com/politica/2011/05/16/actualidad/1305578500_751064.html

Alonso, S. & Kaltwasser, C. R. (2014). Spain: no country for the populist right? *South European Society and Politics.* doi: 10.1080/13608746.2014.985448

Bale, T. (2012). Supplying the insatiable demand: Europe's populist radical right?. *Government & Opposition*, vol. 47, no. 2, 256-274.

Barriere, M., Durgan, A., & Robson, S. (2015). The challenge of *Podemos. International Socialism: A quarterly journal of socialist theory.* 145. Retrieved from http://www.isj.org.uk/index.php4?id=1028&issue=145.

Bescansa, C. (2014, July 18). Presentation. *International Conference of the Asociación de Comunicación Política* (ACOP). Bilbao.

Bollero, D. (2014, 16 August). *Podemos* se consolida como la primera fuerza política en redes sociales. Retrieved from http://www.publico.es/politica/consolida-primera-fuerza-politica-redes.html

Carlin, J. (2015, January 21). Los caballeros de la Mesa Redonda. *El País.* Retrieved 15 February, 2015 from http://politica.elpais.com/politica/2015/01/27/actualidad/1422384264_753104.html

Casals, X. (2013). *El pueblo contra el parlamento. El nuevo populismo en España,* 1989-2013. Madrid: Pasado & Presente.

Castillo, J. (2014). Triangulando el juego: *Podemos*, instituciones y movimientos. *La Hiedra*, 10. http://tinyurl.com/q8vhblk.

CIS (2015, January). Barómetro de enero 2015. Avance de resultados. Estudio no. 3050. Retrieved February 25, 2015 from http://datos.cis.es/pdf/Es3050mar_A.pdf

Cué, C. (2015, February 4). *Podemos* desbanca al PSOE como segunda fuerza política. *El País*. Retrieved February 25, 2015 from http://politica.elpais.com/politica/2015/02/04/actualidad/1423040956_503954.html

Edelman (2014). *2014 Edelman Trust Barometer*. Retrieved from http://www.edelman.com/p/6-a-m/2014-edelman-trust-barometer/

Errejón, I. (2011). Política, conflicto y populismo (I). La construcción discursiva de identidades populares. *Viento sur: Por una izquierda alternative*, 114, 75-84.

Escolar, I. (2015, 1 January). ¿Puede ser ciudadanos el *Podemos* de la derecha? *Diario.es*. Retrieved from http://www.eldiario.es/escolar/Puede-Ciudadanos-Podemos-derecha_6_346175409.html

European Commission (2014). *Standard Eurobarometer 81. Public opinion in the European Union*. Retrieved from http://ec.europa.eu/citizenship/pdf/spring_eurobarometer_july_2014.pdf

Fariza, I. (2014, 2 July). Pablo Iglesias donará el 75% de su salario al programa online La Tuerka. *El País*. Retrieved from http://politica.elpais.com/politica/2014/07/02/actualidad/1404317865_222591.html

Historical Forex Data (March, 2015). Spain's unemployment data: Spain unemployment rate chart. Retrieved from http://ycharts.com/indicators/spain_unemployment_rate_lfs

Inglehart, R. (1999). Trust and well-being in democracy. In M. Warren (ed.). *Democracy and trust* (pp. 88-121). Cambridge: Cambridge University Press.

Institut Balear de Estudios Sociales, (2014, 1 June). *Informe postelectoral Europeas 2014.* Retrieved from http://www.ibesinvestigacion.com/wp-content/uploads/2014/06/120.-anexo-informe-europeas.pdf

Jagers, J. & Walgrave, S. (2007). Populism as political communication style: an empirical study of political parties' discourse in Belgium. *European Journal of Political Research 46* (3), 319-345.

Machuca, P. (2014, 2 February). Entrevista a Pablo Iglesias: "No es izquierda o derecha, es dictadura o democracia". Retrieved from http://www.huffingtonpost.es/2014/02/16/pablo-iglesias-entrevista-podemos_n_4787408.html

Machuca, P. (2014, 27 May). El éxito de *Podemos,* en 5 claves. *El Huffington Post.* Retrieved from http://www.huffingtonpost.es/2014/05/26/podemos-claves-exito_n_5393149.html.

Manetto, F. (2015, 30 April). Monedero dimite de la dirección de *Podemos* tras criticar la estrategia. *El País.* Retrieved from http://politica.elpais.com/politica/2015/04/30/actualidad/1430410083_018713.html

Mudde, C. (2007). *Populist radical right parties in Europe.* Cambridge: Cambridge University Press.

Negrine, R. (2009). *The transformation of political communication.* Basingstoke: Palgrave Macmillan.

Rivas, J. A., & Araque, J. (2004). Aventuras y desventuras del populismo latinoamericano. *Revista de Estudios Políticos,* 124, 229-244.

Rodríguez, G. (2014, 25 May). Cómo han (mal)utilizado Twitter los candidatos. Retrieved from http://www.huffingtonpost.es/2014/05/24/twitter-candidatos-europeos_n_5385659.html

Sanders, K. & Canel, M.J. (2013). *Government communication: cases and challenges.* London: Bloomsbury.

Scammell, M. (2014). *Consumer democracy. The marketing of politics.* Cambridge: Cambridge University Press.

Stobart, L. (2014). Understanding *Podemos* (1/3): 15-M & counter-politics. *Left Flank* (November, 5). http://tinyurl.com/pcfc45t.

Toharia, J.J. (2013, January 10). Científicos y políticos: los polos extremos de la confianza ciudadana. *El País.* Retrieved from http://blogs.elpais.com/metroscopia/2013/01/cientificos-y-politicos-los-polos-extremos-de-la-confianza-ciudadana.html

Warren, M.E. (1999) (ed.) *Democracy and trust.* Cambridge: Cambridge University Press.

Chapter 5

Cosmopolitanism, media and global civil society: From moral to political agency

Peter Dahlgren

Overview

As democracies around the world are generally experiencing long-term trends of declining participation in electoral politics and civil society, we also find an opposite trend: the impressive rise in alternative, extra-parliamentarian political activities (Davis, 2010). While one should be cautious about generalizations, Davis (2010, p.149) notes that these political movements, compared to political parties, tend to address a broader range of issues, offer more opportunity for genuine participation, and are less hierarchical and more inclusive. He has in mind movements that are generally "progressive", which translates into mostly left-reformist, as opposed to right-wing or revolutionary politics. (Yet, he notes that this does not mean that such groups always function in a democratic manner). A major and unprecedented aspect of this activism also tends to engage with issues that cross national borders – their political arena is often global. Moreover, the activists are highly reliant on the web and its various ancillary and mobile platforms.

That many citizens are getting involved in what we might call global civil society, beyond party structures, and especially by using the affordances of these highly sophisticated yet very accessible media technologies, opens a new and unchartered phase in the history of democracy. It also invites many possible lines of inquiry, and scholars are approaching these phenomena from a variety of angles. Here I wish to probe these developments from the standpoint of agency, that is, from the perspective of the meaningfulness of such involvement for the actors involved. How are we to understand the motives, practices, and identities that lead people to engage in the global political arena? My ambition here is to elucidate such agency through the conceptual lens of cosmopolitanism, to see how this may help us to grasp the grounds on which this agency is predicated.

While cosmopolitanism has in recent years become somewhat of a buzzword, it is rather multivalent – like globalization, with which it shares some terrain. So, one task here is to briefly elucidate a few key currents, as well as lines of contestation of the concept. My main focus, however, will be to critically explore what the growing literature on cosmopolitanism says about civic agency in the global arena – a situation where citizenship is in the process of redefining and recreating itself. One of the key currents in this literature, often with an anchoring in the philosophy of Levinas and his understanding of responsibility to the Other, argues for a particular version of citizenship that ultimately rests on conceptions of morality as its platform. The global citizen is thus constructed as a moral agent, one whose agency is defined and (at least implicitly) evaluated according to moral precepts. My response to this is not that it is ill-advised or counter-productive *per se*, but rather that it does not go far enough. To invoke moral frameworks for civic agency and yet ignore the fundamental raison d'être of democratic citizenship – namely as a framework for *political* agency – leaves us in an odd position. Thus I want to probe how we get from moral to political agency, and what the rhetorical issues involved in such a move are.

I will be looking at three thematic areas: first, global civil society as a conceptual setting for political activism, in particular for alternative democratic politics; second, the concept of cosmopolitanism as an important contemporary analytic framework for practice in the global context; and third, global media as a public sphere that can facilitate political participation. Surprisingly, the literature on cosmopolitanism makes few connections with the media; one of the exceptions is Silverstone (2006), and I will make use of his notion of the mediapolis in this regard; he emphasizes the cosmopolitan perspective and treats the individual's media ecology as a habitus for moral and political agency. In the final section, I pull together the discussion with a focus on a trajectory I call civic cosmopolitanism.

Global civil society and alternative politics

Agency, identities, and practices

Why some people become engaged in politics and why many do not are of course complicated questions. One important aspect in this regard is that for people to enact politics, they must in some way feel sufficiently motivated, there must be some normative horizon of the good society, of justice, of a better way, that triggers engagement. Further, they must feel sufficiently empowered, a least at a subjective level, so that participation in politics becomes meaningful for them. Moreover, there must be concrete things for them to do, ways of manifesting this engagement. And there must also be – or they must create – contexts in which to enact their engagement. In short, people need some form of civic identity – a sense of belonging to a political formation that affords them some degree of orientation, efficacy, as well as a sense of possible practices – and the necessary skills – to enact such participation.

Citizenship as an analytic entity has, via an extensive and diverse literature over the past couple of decades, moved beyond its formal and legal horizons to encompass dimensions of agency. The concept is now also understood as referring to the 'doing' of democracy, and this link with agency compels us to reflect on the contexts in which citizenship is enacted, and the contingencies that impact on them.

As a starting point for such considerations, the model of civic cultures (Dahlgren, 2009) can be fruitful. I will not review the entire framework here, but the basic idea is that for people to act politically, there must be sets of cultural resources available to them, to facilitate their agency as citizens. Examining civic cultures helps us to specify the factors that might be facilitating or hindering democratic involvement in any concrete situation. Civic cultures are precarious and vulnerable, yet can also be, when vigorous, empowering. Such civic cultures are shaped by many factors, including structures of power, but even the affordances of the media play a central role.

The civic practices of individuals, groups, and larger collectivities can be routine and recurring (e.g. voting), while others are used less often but can still seen as part of a standard repertoire of practices (e.g., writing letters to representatives, mobilizing, demonstrating). Still others are being invented, adapted, and tested, for example new uses of digital affordances. Communicative skills are central to most civic practices – to be able to read, write, speak – and media technologies have become increasingly central for civic practices. To be able to work with a computer and get around on the internet are important competencies for today's democracy. As new affordances appear with increasing rapidity, new practices are generated. Skills can develop through practices, and in this process foster a sense of empowerment. Civic practices help forge personal and social meaning to the ideals of democracy, and not least help in coalescing forms of civic identities.

What we may call civic identities are a prerequisite for the agency of engaging in politics; and that such identities can be fostered or deflected by the character of civic cultures – which include not least the empowering (and disempowering) potential of media ecologies and media use. There are many ways of being a citizen and of doing democracy; civic identities are protean and multivalent, and evolve via heterogeneous civic cultures in relation to social milieus and institutional mechanisms. Analytically, a robust civic identity implies an empowered political agent and achieved citizenship, one equipped to confront structures of power. Engagement in issues becomes meaningful; citizens feel that they, in concert with others, can in some way make a difference, that they can have some kind of impact on political life, even if they do not win every battle. Today, in the wake of globalization, increasing numbers of people have civic identities and engage in issues that that cross national boundaries.

Situated agency, global issues

Transnational civil society actors vary greatly in their fundamental raison d'être. Some are humanitarian in their orientation; others are engaged in social or cultural networking, for example diasporic or religious groups. Many of these actors are involved in various genres of advocacy, for themselves or as representatives of larger causes or interest groups. A good number of these actors work in tandem with large established international organizations such as the UN or the EU, who actively consult with civil society organizations. Many such actors have become a significant factor at the level of policy-making. There is a large range of explicitly political actors; some give voice to long-standing, protracted conflicts, others air newly emerged ones, while yet others are working politically to alter the behaviour of governments, regulatory bodies or corporations, based on normative visions of global change. For some political actors, religion is a motivational force. When civil society actors turn towards political discussion and debate, they enter into and constitute the public sphere, a theme I will return to below.

In terms of organization, we encounter here the broad terrain of non-governmental organizations (NGOs), non-profit organizations, activist networks, interest and advocacy groups of all kinds, including amorphous social movements. Even alternative journalistic organizations figure here, the most well-known being Indymedia. In short, there is an ever-expanding domain of global civil society, where transnational communication is taking place in a myriad of crisscrossing patterns. Beyond these organizational forms, even grassroots initiatives by activist citizens are part of the overall picture. One of the striking features about all this civic and political global communication is that the range of actors and the breadth of the ideological spectrum visible in global public spheres have become so much larger than they ever were prior to the spread of digital ITCs beginning in the mid-1990s. The literature on global civil society is of course extensive, but some recent contributions which convey summary pictures include Drache (2008); Eberly (2008); Keane (2003); Scholte (2011); Thörn (2009); Walker and Thompson (2008).

Many civil society actors display healthy democratic profiles. Others may have goals or use practices that are questionable, even from within the wide range of definitions and interpretations of democracy that circulate in the world today. Hate groups, racists, and others with obviously anti-democratic and uncivil visions of the world (e.g. terrorist organizations) by definition obviously fall outside the category of global civil society. However, there will no doubt always remain a contested grey zone. One strand of global civil society clearly committed to democratic global development is the alter-globalization movement, also sometimes called the global justice movement, which is comprised of a variety of sub-movements, networks, and organizations. It focuses on a range of issues, such as economic fairness, especially for countries in the global South, environment, human rights, gender issues, labour issues, protection of indigenous cultures, and so on. Though large and diverse, there is a basic conceptual unity, which has to do with the struggles to find counter-hegemonic alternatives to the present trajectory of neoliberal societal development. Over the past decade, the World Social Forum (WSF) and its regional offshoots have served as a major coordinating manifestation of these currents. We can also put the Occupy movement into this camp as well (see Dahlgren, 2013).

These activists are politically on the left, a largely reformist movement seeking to mobilize public opinion and to influence both law makers at different levels as well as corporate actors who are perceived to be doing societal harm in transnational contexts. The WSF has pulled together much of the alter-globalization movement into a loose, overarching organization that also has regional spinoffs, such as the European Social Forum. With participants all over the world, and its roots in the global South, the WSF has a strong non-Western profile. It holds a major annual meeting, with tens of thousands participating; these began in Brazil as a counterpoint to the Davos meetings of global political and economic elites. The meetings seek to globally coordinate, build alliances, share knowledge and experiences, and develop strategies. The alter-globalization movement generally, and the WSF in particular, has been made academically visible in recent years; see, for example, Acosta (2009); Gills (2011); Hosseini (2010); Maeckelburgh (2009); Pleyers (2011).

Activism in global civil society has usually been seen as a one of many other currents of globalization, but more recently another term has also come to the fore as an analytic frame: cosmopolitanism. Let us see what lies behind this concept.

Cosmopolitanism: ways of seeing and being

The notion of cosmopolitanism is of course quite old; even Socrates famously claimed that he was not an Athenian, nor a Greek, but a citizen of the world. Kant gave the concept a strong ethical dimension in his modern version of the world citizen; this element remains prominent even today, as the concept is being reinvented. With the continuing integration of the world via the processes of globalization – albeit often in very uneven, unequal and contested ways – the Other, or rather the many Others, all come closer to us in our everyday lives. On one level we can see cosmopolitanism as an expression of concern for the Other, transferred to global contexts.

More specifically – and more useful for research – cosmopolitanism offers an analytic frame for approaching issues about social perceptions of and relations with distant others in the world; it helps us to illuminate the normative grounds for such practices. Morality, as the fundamental conceptions of right and wrong in human affairs – and ethics, as the application, or codification, of morality into concrete norms of behaviour – constitute, at the bottom, the foundation of most human action, even if only implicitly. It therefore remains an important analytic angle of vision for understanding the social world under globalized modernity, not least in the context of transnational politics and political communication.

Multiple horizons

In the rapidly growing literature on cosmopolitanism, we find a number of emphases. One important line of inquiry addresses the vision of a more just and democratic world order (e.g. Archibugi, 2008; Gould, 2004; Sullivan & Kymlicka, 2007; Vernon, 2010). Among such authors, Held (2010) is a prominent voice, and he asserts the exhaustion of traditional politics, especially in the face of massive global problems such as climate change, the financial crisis, and human rights. He argues that cosmopolitanism is the only realistic way forward. Others focus on a particular aspect of this larger theme, namely the notion of citizenship, and the issues of rights and inclusion in the contemporary global situation, not least in regard to the EU (e.g. Benhabib, 2004, 2006; Habermas, 2006; Morris, 2010).

Further, much of the contemporary discussion about cosmopolitanism ranges over moral theory and political philosophy (Breckenridge, *et al.*, 2004; Brock & Brighouse, 2005; Nussbaum, 2006). These contributions are to a great extent characterized by normative discourses. Still other interventions address the socio-cultural preconditions for cosmopolitanism and/or its subjective dimensions (e.g., Beck, 2006; Appiah, 2007; Hannerz, 1996). In her recent review of the literature, Taraborrelli (2015) distinguishes between moral, legal, and cultural forms of cosmopolitanism. While some of the authors link cosmopolitanism in a general way with the political, a few explicitly frame it in terms of a critical confrontation with neoliberalism and its consequences (e.g. Cheah, 2007; Dallmayr, 2009; Delanty, 2009; and Harvey, 2009). Indeed, Harvey takes several authors, such as Nussbaum, Beck and Held, to task for what he sees to be their implicit collusion with neoliberalism. The collection by Braidotti, Hanafin, and Blaagaard (2013) also puts the emphasis on what is called cosmopolitics, while the anthology by Carus and Parvu (2014) underscores how resistance to global hegemonies might contribute to new ways of conceiving cosmopolitanism that avoid totalizing and (ultimately) hegemonic approaches.

Delanty (2009) sees cosmopolitanism as a dimension in contemporary social processes that can serve as a normative critique of globalization, and thus of capitalism. He underscores that cosmopolitanism can promote our capacity for self-reflection, and foster new ways of seeing the world when diverse peoples experience common problems. Distancing himself from more anthropological approaches, he argues that the conflicts around 'difference' in the world today are less about culture and more about social and economic questions that have significant political implications. The global world requires a new kind of imagination, i.e. one that is cosmopolitan and where the learning process is about becoming both post-national and post-market in one's horizons. Thus, cosmopolitanism can be seen as promoting changes in the understanding between Self and Other, and projecting this motif onto the global arena. His framework includes a micro-level of identities, social movements and communities, where new cultural forms can take shape and new spaces of discourse can open up – to confront political realities.

In the pluralism of approaches to cosmopolitanism, we see a fundamental issue that has to do with the basic tension between universalism and the particular (or local, or national). Is there one set of cosmopolitan values and perceptions, a 'one-size-fits-all'? The answers have political implications. Breckenridge *et al.* (2002) propose that the concept be used in the plural, and not be associated with the unitary, privileged position of the European tradition, since the motivation and capacity to reflect on those beyond one's own culture is to be found in all regions of the world. At the same time, the editors suggest that that a genuine 'spirit' of cosmopolitanism is something that is yet in the future, and should be treated as a normative vision. Thus, we can discern an unresolved tension between, on the one hand, cosmopolitanism as an expression of multiple empirical realities around the world, and, on the other, cosmopolitanism as a unitary global ideal, with universalist virtues (these tensions are followed up in Brock 2013). Universalist claims are at times vulnerable to critiques of embodying ethnocentrism or cultural specificity (e.g. Habermas' notions about the ideal speech situation). Is the notion of a unitary normative vision inherently an expression of a camouflaged manoeuvre for cultural power?

Turner (2002) draws on the 16th century writer Michel Montaigne and his sceptical humanism, especially his notion of irony, to develop precisely a sense of universal cosmopolitan virtue. Turner sees Montaigne as espousing what he calls the softer (feminine) values of mercy, compassion and tenderness – in response to the horrors of the wars of his time. Cosmopolitan virtue basically encompasses pacifist values that preclude violence and promote human agency and dignity. Turner argues that there is a great diversity of human happiness, but there is unity in suffering. For cosmopolitan virtue, a "general opposition to human suffering constitutes a standpoint that both transcends and unites different cultures and historical epochs" (Turner, 2002: xx).

If human rights exist to protect us from suffering, then there are universal human obligations to oppose misery, to respect cultures of other peoples and to oppose governments that fail to protect human rights. Turner makes the cosmopolitan argument even more convincing by contending that the vulnerability of the human body provides a starting point for an account of human commonality and compassion as the basis for a cosmopolitan ethic. For him, The UN Declaration of Human Rights is obviously a very cosmopolitan document, which he builds into his argument.

Thus, one way of understanding contemporary cosmopolitanism is to see it as a response to ethnic cleansing and racial violence in the context of a global economy that is creating ever-greater gulfs between rich and poor. Such a virtue is a set of obligations that flows from a recognition of the vulnerability of persons and of the precariousness of institutions with the globalization of culture. Turner thereby takes a clear stand against moral relativism. However, one could respond that Turner's position is 'easy': to reduce physical suffering is perhaps not so controversial. In situations that, for example, have to do with expressions of minority community membership in majoritarian cultural settings (e.g. apparel of religious expression), can we easily identify an operational universal ethic?

Towards empirical investigation

Given the conceptual fluidity of the literature on cosmopolitanism, there is of course the danger that the notion can become all things to all people. Corpus Ong (2009) discusses how theorists in various disciplines view the central idea of cosmopolitanism, and he derives four basic categories, under which he places the major authors: *closed* (i.e. un- or anti-cosmopolitan), *prestige* (where status and privilege are closely associated with it), *banal* (an everyday, 'ordinary' openness to otherness as an expression of one's own identity) and *ecstatic* (a kind of visionary enthusiasm). Quite a number of authors land in the latter category. Other reflections on the literature, such as Kendall, Woodward and Skribis (2009), note a certain degree of political naïveté among many authors. There is a utopian tendency to construct a new world of tolerant and responsible citizens, while offering little analytic insight on how to deal with the major global divides – or ignoring them altogether. These authors thus share some of Harvey's (2009) critical views in this regard.

Further, Skrbis and Woodward (2013) suggest that many discussions on cosmopolitanism would be more fruitful if the ethical component were a bit more modest, and if the concept could be developed with a stronger eye on methodology. They find that that 'ordinary cosmopolitanism' is expressed as an ensemble of discourses mobilized as everyday accounts. These accounts deal with such issues as cultural heterogeneity and global problems. However, rather than taking the 'high road' which leads to openness and hospitality to strangers, and puts generalized human needs ahead of national interests, many people instead discursively frame cosmopolitanism as the attractive affordances of globalization, such as travel and culinary diversity. Moreover, even discourses about 'cultural loss' and the 'dilution of national culture' are in circulation.

While their research underscores the obvious point that cosmopolitanism is as yet not a universal phenomenon, it also – and more interestingly – suggests that it is also possible to empirically study the concept as something socially constructed by concrete actors, contingent on specific contexts. Also, their work affirms the importance of Delanty's idea that cosmopolitanism is also played out (or not) in the everyday terrain of identities and communities (see also Hier, 2008). Here, we can readily see the ideals of cosmopolitanism in tension with concrete multicultural settings, not least around the issues of immigration. They emphasize that cosmopolitanism is something big, but must also be manifested in small contexts; an immense global intellectual and political project.

One does not have to be physically mobile to be a cosmopolitan, as demonstrated by Kant himself, who seldom ventured far beyond Köningsberg. Hannerz (1996) underscores that cosmopolitanism has to do with a mind-set, a disposition. And increasingly, the world is coming to us: more and more often, the local manifests elements of the global (e.g. mixed neighbourhoods). Cosmopolitanism, as an 'openness to the world' according to Corpus Ong (2009) can in principle begin on one's own street. And not least, we have access to the 'world', via the media, as will be discussed presently. Sociological common sense would suggest that having contact with those different from oneself could help facilitate a cosmopolitan stance. Certainly the world – present and past – is full of examples of successful neighbourhoods, cities, states and empires where tolerance and openness to difference have prevailed.

However, the socio-cultural prerequisites are rather high, and it is not surprising that the empirical results such as offered by Skrbis and Woodward (2013) are quite sobering. Self-reflection with respect to our own cultural context, origins, and values, which go hand in hand with scepticism towards the 'grand narratives' of modern ideologies (Turner, 2002), seemingly involve a considerable degree of cultural capital. Achieving a sense of distance from one's own background and identity, developing some critical distance about the ultimate authority of one's own culture, are not ingrained dimensions of most collective frames of reference.

This kind of cultural capital, predicated on routine encounters with those significantly different from oneself, is precisely what many insular communities lack the world over, not least those in a minority or subordinate position. Getting even a 'small taste' of globalization via the media, for example, may in fact lead to further cultural defensiveness, closure, exclusion, and even violence.

Intersections: post-colonialism

In considering these aspects, especially in regard to identities, it is important that we do not lapse into a dead-end quest for some mythic"new cosmopolitan subject". Rather, we need to underscore what Dallmayr (2003) calls the "situated differences and motivational resources" in discussing empirically the socio-cultural contingencies of cosmopolitan practices and identities. This angle soon touches base with the themes of history and power. While culture in today's world is of course not something that simply mirrors the flow of economic and political power from centres to peripheries, the history of colonialism makes it difficult to deny the importance of these mechanisms (and here of course the structures of the media and the patterns of their representation loom especially large). In short, if globalization constitutes the key contemporary condition for the actualization of cosmopolitanism, then the prevailing power relations (and their historical origins) in the global arena would seemingly have importance for understanding the character and possibilities of cosmopolitanism. Global power can of course be approached in different ways, not least the political economy of the world system, but the perspective of post-colonialism offers a significant prism through which to view cosmopolitanism. Post- colonialism, in ways similar to Cultural Studies (with which it at times blends together), is sensitive to how culture and the production of meaning are always bound up in some way or other with relations of power.

It is interesting to note that in the past two decades or so two key theoretic traditions – globalization (with its home largely in the social sciences) and post-colonialism (hovering more in the humanities) have had relatively few encounters with each other. They seemingly exist in parallel universes, when in fact they should be very much entwined – although this lack of interaction is beginning to be addressed (for example, see the collection by Krishnaswamy and Hawley, 2008). For cosmopolitanism, post-colonialism can serve to help alert us to the historical antecedents of a vast array of aspects where power, especially cultural power, has relevance: patterns of cultural influences, images of the other, identity processes, integration/assimilation, language use, institution-building, and so on. Conceptually and empirically, cosmopolitanism cannot be reduced to a mere function of power, yet nor can power be ignored. If power is not obviously manifest, then is always hovering there – in both micro- and macro- circumstances – as a potential on the threshold of becoming realized. Power evokes counter-power, so it is not simply a case of uni-directional and deterministic mechanisms, even though hegemonic positions are prevalent.

Pulling together the key trajectories in the literature on cosmopolitanism for the discussion at hand, we see that the concept is quite multivalent, yet a critical strain can be extracted, one that resonates with the contributions of post-colonialist studies and that can be deployed in the confrontations with global neoliberalism. There is a strong normative dimension; while this can be veer off into excessive philosophical enthusiasm about a new world order, it also anchors a responsibility to the Other, to global Others. While tensions remain between situated and universalist versions of cosmopolitanism, there is sufficient ground for a view that resonates with the discourses of human rights and the imperative to reduce human suffering.

Increasingly, the global world is becoming part of our spaces of habitat, part of our everyday encounters, in physical or mediated terms. Cosmopolitan mind-sets, and the identities and practices that embody them, have socio-cultural contingencies; empirical research suggests that for most people in most settings, the cultural capital or other resources required for the necessary self-reflection and distancing regarding the prevailing collective world views are insufficient. In practice, then, we may expect cosmopolitanism to be associated with groups who are in some ways specialized or privileged. With these general precepts in place, let us now turn to the next theme of the discussion, the media, and in particular, the global *mediapolis.*

The *mediapolis*: a new kind of public sphere

I mentioned at the outset that analyses of the media have oddly not figured extensively in the literature on cosmopolitanism. There are some exceptions, among them Norris and Ingelhart (2009), who offer a major empirical effort to establish the links between mass media use and cosmopolitan mind-sets. Large-scale international surveys on values suggest a general positive correlation with media use in this regard, in most countries, although polarization is also a consequence. The authors underscore, however, the research complexity of establishing causal relationships, and make the point that there are also many non-media variables at work. More focused efforts are found in Boltanski (1999), who addresses in a theoretic manner the theme of recognizing and identifying with distant others via news coverage of suffering, and Chouliaraki (2006), who addresses this theme but in a more rigorously empirical manner. Robertson (2010, 2015) takes a broad look at television news, its journalists/editors, and its viewers around the world. She elucidates the role of television news, of both mainstream and 'counter-hegemonic' variants, in fostering cosmopolitan horizons. For my purposes here, I will make use of Silverstone (2006), since it explicitly engages with key themes in the literature on cosmopolitanism in its conceptualization of the media's role.

On the *mediapolis*

The book's style is more essayistic than empirical, and has more the normative character of the dominant literature on cosmopolitanism. However, it assumes that the media play a decisive role in the constitution of late modernity and its forms of globalization. It provides a useful starting point for some reflections on media and cosmopolitanism, with a focus on their relationship to democracy. I want to sketch his basic ideas pertaining to cosmopolitanism as a necessary element for civic agency in the modern globalized world, and the character of the media as a precondition for such agency. I will thus be using Silverstone's discussion on media and morality as a springboard for conceptually preparing the way for an understanding of cosmopolitanism that links up with democratic agency and practice in global contexts.

Silverstone navigates carefully between optimism and pessimism, yet he is clearly conveying an ambitious vision; unsurprisingly, Corpus Ong (2009) unambiguously places him as an ecstatic proponent of cosmopolitanism. Silverstone adroitly balances the tension between one or many cosmopolitanisms: he pushes strongly for generalized shared ethics of responsibility to the Other, but adamantly acknowledges the situated character of such ethics, i.e. that people's actions and moral frameworks are contingent upon their circumstances. Such contingency inevitably impacts on the meaning and efficacy of action. He argues that media today have imposed conditions of cosmopolitanism on us: we can – and must – respond accordingly from the standpoint of our own lives. Not least, he is very much aware of the significance of power relations, especially in regard to the institutions and functioning of the media. This ushers us into the realm of democracy and civic agency. However, let us first backtrack and briefly summarize his main points.

He begins with two familiar observations: that globalization, in all of its economic, cultural, social, and political dimensions, is a key feature of late modernity, and that the media play a decisive role in this regard. Moreover, the media are becoming what he calls 'environmental'; they no longer can be seen as simply discrete flows of messages or information, but rather take on the character of dense symbolic ecologies that penetrate just about every corner of our existence. From these premises he arrives at an important thesis: the *mediapolis* is the space of mediated global appearances. It is via the media that the world appears to us and where appearance constitutes the world. It is through the media that we learn who we are – and who we are different from, and where relations between self and other are conducted in a global public arena. The media establish connections, relationships; they position us in the world.

The *mediapolis* is both a normative and an empirical term. Empirically, it is something other than a rational Habermasian public sphere; it is cacophonic, with multiple voices, inflections images, and rhetoric – it resides beyond logic and rationality, and it cannot offer any expectation of fully effective communication. The communications dynamic that Silverstone sees here he calls *contrapunctual* (from Edward Said's notion of counterpoint). Each communicative thread gains significance only in relationship to others – together, the ensemble of tension-ridden, contradictory communicative interventions comprises the whole.

Normatively, however, despite differences in communicative and other forms of power, the *mediapolis* demands mutual responsibility between producers and audiences/receivers, as well as a capacity for reflexivity on the part of all involved, including recognition of cultural differences. This raises issues of the kinds of reality created by the *mediapolis*, the kinds of publicness, who appears – and how – as well as who does not appear. The notion of *mediapolis* is thus a challenge, a challenge to inequities of representation, mechanisms of exclusion, the imbalances of media power (via both state and capital), and "the ideological and prejudicial frames of unreflexive reporting and storytelling" (Silverstone, 2006: p. 37). Thus, the media, in their representations of the world, inevitably engage in what he calls boundary work. This is done at the macro-level of larger ideological classifications, but also at the micro-level, in the continuous inscription of difference in any and every media text or discourse. Boundaries are constantly being drawn, reinforced, and altered between various constellations of Us and Them.

The imperative of moral response

Public space is inexorably political, and the media play a big role in the formation of social and civic space, as we know. A key argument in Roger Silverstone's book is that media also constitute a *moral* space – that is, they are a significant site for the construction of a *moral order.* This moral order gives rise to the issue of proximity and distance in regard to the people and events portrayed in the media. Silverstone affirms the importance of – and often the difficulty of establishing what is – 'proper distance' in regard to the way the media situate us in relation to what is portrayed. Social distance is a moral category; to establish proper distance involves a search for enough knowledge and understanding of the other person or the other culture to enable response, responsibility and care; it requires some imagination. The *mediapolis,* then, requires a moral response from us. Silverstone has in his sights a kind of 'moral minimalism' – even though we may still find the normative admonishment involved here to be quite ambitious. Moral response in this context is predicated on the cognitive capacity to understand human difference and sameness, to be able to live with ambiguity in an ever-changing world, and the capacity to respond in a basic, humane way. While he speaks of moral minimalism, Silverstone allows for a variety of responses, i.e. different forms of cosmopolitan behaviour.

This moral response is expressed in our responsibility for thinking, speaking, listening and acting. Silverstone in fact claims that the conditions of the *mediapolis* can provide us with resources for judgement – for cognitive, aesthetic, and moral judgement (for example, the role of the fourth estate includes a version of the Enlightenment project), including the judgement of proper distance. This notion of the responsibility towards others is inspired in part by Levinas (as it is in much of the current literature on cosmopolitanism). Responsibility requires self-reflection; without it we can fail in our responsibility, and we end up "being a partner in evil". Silverstone admits that to speak of virtue may sound a bit quaint today, but we really have no other option.

In underscoring the significance of morality and ethics, Silverstone does not simply mean we should "moralize" about the media, but rather that moral dimensions should become a focus of analytic concern, just as social, political, cultural perspectives are part of our analytic approach to the media. Our responsibility, our moral response to the *mediapolis*, is of course shaped to some extent by the media themselves. Chouliaraki (2006), for example, explores how different modes of media representation can position us differently – evoke different kinds of response – to the suffering portrayed in television journalism. There is clearly an element of media power here: definitional control lies most immediately with the news organizations, but Silverstone's position here is to emphasize that there is still responsibility on both sides. Journalists, editors, and producers have a responsibility for the representations they offer, while audiences/users have an obligation to reflect on what they encounter and respond in an ethical manner – both to the world portrayed and towards the media.

Adding online media

While Silverstone's book was published in 2006, he hardly makes mention of online media, which is puzzling. Not only was Web 2.0 in full swing at the time, but also the interactive dimension of the web, beyond the largely one-way model of the mass media, in fact offers more potential for precisely the kind of moral engagement he is advocating. Here, we can take some help from a recent book on the global public sphere by Volkmer (2014). While noting that the familiar, technical macro-networks of communication – with their active audience-users – constitute a premise for contemporary global communication, she emphasizes the multi-level character of these media and their communicative modes. She underscores that the character of globalized communication today is not defined by these media structures in themselves, but rather by the actual way that individuals and organizations communicate across diverse platforms, from all manner of mainstream media to all kinds of social media. It is in the communication – and editing, mixing, filtering, modifying – of content that we find the new global sphere.

This new public sphere is shaped by individualized nodes "situated within a universe of subjective, personal networked structures linking individuals across world regions" (p.1). There is thus a significant emphasis on subjective dynamics here, not only in terms of communicative processes, but in the very character of 'lived' public spaces. Volkmer uses the concept of "micro-networks" to capture the interdependent connections between actors across these thus "assembled" communicative spaces. We have thereby left behind the defining framework of nation-states, and moved to a regime where the local blends readily with the global and all stops in between, based on the identities, loyalties, and allegiances of the actors, operating across the full range of media technologies and platforms; this global public sphere operates across supra- and subnational societal contexts. Adding this portrait of global digital communication renders the notion of the *mediapolis* all the more compelling. Each citizen has all the more potential to be a participating actor, who makes moral choices.

With mediated globalization, the status of the cosmopolitan thus re-emerges as a theme of central concern. Historically, cosmopolitanism has mostly been associated with, or an attribute of, certain elite strata of society. Today, the symbolic global connections via the media raise this to the level of common concern, and allow for extensive participation. In the modern world linked by the media, we are all positioned in relation to remote others. Silverstone asserts the importance of cosmopolitanism, yet is quick to point out the difficulties. It can have a romantic ring to it and can be interpreted in different ways; it embodies a commitment to both reflexivity and toleration. It obligates us to be open to the stranger – even the stranger in oneself. Still more problematically, it remains unclear how these moral horizons can be connected with concrete political practices.

Towards civic cosmopolitanism

From morality to the political

In all this, Silverstone admits that we have some obvious and difficult questions to deal with, not least conceptually. The public as such does not have a strong meaningful status, and, we might add, empirically it is not politically very efficacious. Thought, speech, and action are disconnected and compromised by absence of context, memory, and analytic rigour, as well as by deficit of trust. Also, we witness patterns of withdrawal from the public realm, into the private; in fact, the major dilemmas confronting democracy are exacerbated in the global context. Silverstone's reflections on the political go well beyond traditional liberalism as understood in political philosophy, which underscores individuals' rights and their pursuit of private happiness. His is a political sensibility that puts him at home with republicanism, with its emphasis on individual development through democratic engagement and social responsibilities.

Thus, the *mediapolis* becomes the site not only for moral response, but, potentially, for practices. His notion that our responsibility is expressed in thinking, speaking, listening, and acting leads us directly to the themes of civic agency and skills. The cosmopolitan moral agent must move beyond the state of merely thinking about his or her responsibility; it must be enacted, embodied via some kind of action (which, in the context of the political, will often take some form of communication). Such proactive social ethics, that demand engagement with and responsibility for global others, point us towards cosmopolitan citizenship, which engages with the world not least via the *mediapolis,* in a manner that is strongly tied to some version of democracy. This link between cosmopolitanism and democratic civic agency – I call it *civic cosmopolitanism* (Dahlgren 2013) – involves translating the cosmopolitan moral stance into concrete political contexts that benefit not just our own interests but those of globalized others. Cosmopolitanism becomes thus an inexorable dimension of contemporary republican civic virtue and agency.

I share Silverstone's view of the media as environmental, as an ecology that can become – or has already become – in part become "polluted" (in a moral sense) in many areas and thus detrimental to our well-being. Silverstone is concerned with fundamental questions of how we should live – and live with all our Others. He is concerned with the "good society", or rather, the "good, globalized society". It is here, in a sense at the outer edges of his work, where I would like to pick up that baton and run with it.

In talking about the media, Silverstone tends to foreground the mass media, and argues that they contain institutions and organizations, which in turn are comprised of categories of people working in their identifiable roles under specific situations: journalists, editors of various sorts, owners, producers, programme directors, managers, accountants, lawyers, etc.

As I mentioned earlier, he does not develop the discussion much on the internet, although he underscores that its technologies are altering the basic parameters of the *mediapolis* and points out that in terms of publicness, the internet (or at least small scale interaction on the net) requires the mass media as a context, as a contextual background, to avoid spiralling away into enclave mentalities (though we would add that the internet itself of course also has the character of mass mediated communication). Let us add the horizons of the digital global public sphere I referred to above, as developed by Volkmer (2014), with its emphasis on personal networks that link individuals – netizens – globally. We thus have a situation today where global netizens are technologically empowered to impact on the character of the *mediapolis.* In short, we have sets of individuals who act as elements of larger collective agencies, as well as in looser social networks. I would emphasize that this horizon of the individual level does not to signal a suspension of a sociological perspective, but rather underscores the dimension of human agency, where moral reflection is in principle always possible. Thus, in simple terms, the *mediapolis* is populated by people acting as audience members, as participants in the media industries, and as netizens. The differing horizons of these various social positions of course provide different contexts in terms of moral action.

The horizon of civic agency

Cosmopolitanism, in ways similar to the dilemmas of late modern democracy, involves realistic balances between optimism and pessimism, as well as between global and local loyalties. Also, we have tensions between notions of a universalistic democratic core and recognition of plural modes of doing democracy in the world. Few would claim that cosmopolitan citizens must be free-floating in terms of their loyalties, but certainly globalization, with its acceleration of mobility and communication, has thrust democracy into an age where it can no longer be conceived exclusively in terms of national boundaries. However, the jet-set citizen with no anchoring in any particular place will probably not easily respond with moral engagement to the difficult circumstances of remote Others. To be a cosmopolitan citizen does not entail being devoid of a “home”, nor does it require that one abandons all sense of solidarity towards one's country and its people. Without such an anchoring, civic practices will lack grounding. Even in the context of democracy, it is no doubt the case that empathy begins – and is learned – at home.

So, the issue at bottom becomes to conceptualize the transition from moral response to civic agency, to embody cosmopolitan morality in some kind of concrete political practice. Moral response can be seen as a form of engagement, a subjective pre-requisite for political participation (Dahlgren, 2009). And here, the media as sites and spaces for civic practices – as the *mediapolis* – take on obvious relevance.

As a first step, it is worth reiterating a degree of caution, or at least modesty, in regard to universalisms. Turner's (2002) anchoring in the horizons of human rights is an indispensable element here, but things can and do get more complex. Dallmayr (2003) argues cogently that an excessive emphasis on moral universalism can precisely lead us to ignore the contingency of situated differences, external constraints, and other factors that shape the specificity of human action. As he says, "...it is insufficiently moral – in fact, it is hardly moral at all – to celebrate universal values everywhere without also seeking to enable and empower people in their different settings and locations". (Dallmayr, 2003, p. 438). Even if we accept universal norms and ethics at a theoretic level, they do not translate automatically into practice, but require interpretation and application. This immediately gives rise to political questions: how do we make such interpretations and translations?

He offers an important conceptual step in this regard: the "promotion of justice – that is, the removal of misery and oppression – falls more heavily on the rich and powerful than it does on the poor, the oppressed, the subaltern". (Dallmayr 2003, p. 438) From this it seems that the signposts point in the direction of a politics aimed at enhancing freedom and self-governance, i.e. the deepening and strengthening of democracy – allowing, even here, that local circumstances and traditions will inevitably frame this conceptual ideal in various ways. We understand that there are very different structures, dynamics and degrees of normative expectations involved, as Archibugi (2008) argues. This suggests, not least, that at the global level, we launch ourselves into a disappointing dead-end if we visualize world democracy as developing from simple extension of national structures into the transnational arena.

Likewise, we lay aside the idea of the emergence of a new kind of universal "cosmopolitan citizens" or "global souls" who will inhabit the nations of the world and politically lead them towards a more harmonious order on the planet. This scenario is similar to the futile vision of the united workers of the world. We have to be alert and sensitive to the specific settings and the conditions of potential civic agency. Such agency must always be anchored in one's own immediate realities, yet together with that demanding mindset that we somehow cannot bypass, namely some reflexive capacity to distance oneself from these realities, to understand how they impinge on possible forms of practice. In short, what is required is a balancing act: we need to downsize our visions to remove them from the realm of fantasy, yet keep them sufficiently larger than life so that they can still inspire.

If we translate these reflections in the real global political world using, for example, the issue of the environmental dangers that threaten the planet, we have here an overwhelming cosmopolitan imperative. Here, in fact, ultimately, a concern for the Other equals a concern for us all, including ourselves. Each of us has a responsibility to all the global Others for the ecological health of the world. Yet, in the present dangerous ecological situation, it is clear that any moral universalism in regard to the environment must be translated into concrete strategies at regional, national, and local levels – while at the same time maintaining global coordination. We cannot consume our way forward to better ecological balance (despite what some corporate interests would like us to believe), nor is it sufficient that we each individually sort our garbage, although that can be of help. What is required are massive, globally linked efforts to alter fundamental patterns of production, consumption, and lifestyles; we need to arrive at a historical turning point in our contemporary civilization. These efforts, in turn, require political work, at all levels.

Civic agency must deal with structures, and one of the problems of the transnational arena is, as noted, precisely the thinness of democratic structures out there. Habermas (2006) and Benhabib (2006), for example, each draw the conclusion that transnational civic activism today involves the struggle to establish legal frameworks to defend democratic principles in the global arena. Within Europe, this translates, for them, into the EU as a significant project – while acknowledging the issues of the EU's relationship to the rest of the world (e.g. "fortress Europe"). Not only can civic cosmopolitanism not ignore global structures, it must actively struggle to develop them and give them a democratic character. For others, such as many of the groups united under the alter-globalization umbrella of the WSF, it requires instead trying to institutionalize the thin presence of democratic global civil society into more robust, durable structures.

If the socio-cultural prerequisites for civic cosmopolitanism are quite high, we should not be startled to learn that in the West, its actors tend to come from the educated middle classes. Yet, in the global South, the pattern seems more heterogeneous. Certainly many of the activists come from privileged backgrounds, but others do not. They instead can be seen as specialized, rather than privileged in this context. The contingencies that facilitate their participation as civic cosmopolitans have more to do with their ability to analyse the connections between local and global circumstances, the counter-hegemonic discourses they encounter, the sense of empowerment engendered by their engagement. In other words, it would seem that the direct experience of the political can in some settings play a more decisive role in mobilizing engagement in global issues than factors such as education or economic background. Moreover, their empowerment as netizens via the online technologies of the *mediapolis* has arguably had in comparative terms even more impact than in the West.

Nobody said it would be easy, but we seem to have run out of global alternatives if we value both our own survival and something that we can still call democracy. Democratic civic agency needs to incorporate the cosmopolitan perspective and pay more attention to morality as an analytic dimension for understanding political agency as an expression of subjectivity. Cosmopolitanism needs to analytically further engage with the media, and look beyond moral categories to situated political practices. Thus: civic cosmopolitans, unite! But do so in your own political contexts. And use the *mediapolis.*

Bibliography

Acosta, R. (2009). *NGO and social movement networking in the World Social Forum: an anthropological approach.* Saarbrücken: VDM Verlag.

Archibugi, D. (2008). *The global commonwealth of citizens: towards a cosmopolitan democracy.* Princeton and Oxford: Princeton University Press.

Appiah, K. A. (2007). *Cosmopolitanism: ethics in a world of strangers.* New York: Norton.

Bauman, Z. (1998). *Globalization: the human consequences.* New York: Columbia University Press.

Beck, U. (2006). *The cosmopolitan vision.* Oxford: Blackwell.

Benhabib, S. (2006). *Another cosmopolitanism.* New York: Oxford University Press.

Benhabib, S. (2004). *The rights of others: aliens, residents and citizens.* Cambridge: Cambridge University Press.

Boltanski, L. (1999). *Distant suffering: morality, media and politics.* Cambridge: Cambridge University Press.

Braidotti, R., Hanafin, P., & Blaagaard, B. B. (eds.)(2013). *After cosmopolitanism.* Abingdon: Routledge.

Breckenridge, C. A., Pollock, S., Bhabha, H. K. & Chakrabarty, D. (eds.) (2002) *Cosmopolitanism.* Durham and London: Duke University Press.

Brock, G., (ed.) (2013). *Cosmopolitanism versus non-cosmopolitanism: critiques, defenses, reconceptualizations.* Oxford: Oxford University Press.

Brock, G. & Brighouse, H. (eds.) (2005). *The political philosophy of cosmopolitanism.* London: Cambridge University Press.

Carus, T. & Parvu, C. A. (eds.) (2014). *Cosmopolitanism and the legacies of dissent.* Abingdon: Routledge.

Cheah, P. (2007). *Inhuman conditions: on cosmopolitanism and human rights.* Cambridge, MA and London: Harvard University Press.

Chouliaraki, L. (2006). *The spectatorship of suffering.* London: Sage Publications.

Corpus Ong, J. (2009). The cosmopolitan continuum: locating cosmopolitanism in media and cultural studies. *Media, Culture & Society,* 31(3), 449-466.

Dahlgren, P. (2009). *Media and political engagement: citizens, communication, and democracy.* New York: Cambridge University Press.

Dahlgren, P. (2013). *The political web: participation, media, and alternative democracy.* Basingstoke: Palgrave.

Dallmayr, F. (2003). Cosmopolitanism: moral and political. *Political Theory* 31 (3) 421-442.

Davis, A. (2010). *Political communication and social theory.* Abingdon: Routledge.

Delanty, G. (2009). *The cosmopolitan imagination: the renewal of critical social theory.* Cambridge: Cambridge University Press.

Drache, D. (2008). *Defiant publics: the unprecedented reach of the global citizen.* Cambridge: Polity Press.

Eberly, D. E. (2008). *The rise of global civil society: building communities and nations from the bottom up.* New York: Encounter Books.

Giddens, A. (1999). *Runaway world – how globalisation is reshaping our lives.* London: Profile Books.

Gills, B. K. (ed.) (2011). *Globalization and the global politics of justice.* London: Routledge.

Godrej, F. (2011). *Cosmopolitan political thought: method, practice, discipline.* New York: Oxford University Press.

Gould, C. C. (2004). *Globalizing democracy and human rights.* New York: Cambridge University Press.

Habermas, J. (2006). *The divided west.* Cambridge:Polity.

Hannerz, U. (1996). *Transnational connections: culture, people, places.* London: Routledge.

Harvey, D. (2009). *Cosmopolitanism and the geographies of freedom.* New York: Columbia University Press.

Held, D. (2010). *Cosmopolitanism.* Cambridge: Polity Press.

Hier, S. P. (2008) Transformative democracy in the age of second modernity: cosmopolitanization, communicative agency and the reflexive subject. *New Media & Society* 10 (1) 27-44.

Hosseini, H. S.A. (2010). *Alternative globalizations: an integrative approach to studying dissident knowledge in the global justice movement.* London: Routledge.

Kendall, G., Woodward, I. & Skribis, Z. (2009). *The sociology of cosmopolitanism: globalization, identity, culture and government.* Basingstoke: Palgrave Macmillan.

Krishnaswamy, R. & Hawley, J. C. (eds.) (2008). *The postcolonial and the global.* Minneapolis: The University of Minnesota Press.

Maeckelburgh, M. (2009). *The will of the many: how the alterglobalisation movement is changing the face of democracy.* London: Pluto Press.

Morris, L. (2010). *Aslylum, welfare and the cosmopolitan ideal: a sociology of rights.* Abingdon: Routledge.

Norris, P. & Ingelhart, R. (2009). *Cosmopolitan communications: cultural diversity in a globalized world.* Cambridge: Cambridge University Press.

Nussbaum, M. (2006). *Frontiers of justice: disability, nationality and species membership.* Cambridge, Mass.: Belknap Press.

Pleyers, G. (2011). *Alter-Globalization: becoming actors in a global age.* Cambridge: Polity Press.

Robertson, A. (2010). *Mediated cosmopolitanism: the world of television news.* Camridge: Polity Press.

Robertson, A. (2015). *Global news: reporting conflicts and cosmopolitanism.* New York: Peter Lang.

Scholte, J. A. (ed.) (2011). *Building global democracy: civil society and accountable global governance.* Cambridge: Cambridge University Press.

Silverstone, R. (2006). *Media and morality: on the rise of the mediapolis.* Cambridge: Polity.

Skrbis, Z. & Woodward, I. (2013). *Cosmopolitanism: uses of the idea.* London: Sage.

Sullivan. W. M. & Kymlicka,W. (eds.) (2007). *The globalisation of ethics.* New York: Cambridge University Press.

Taraborrelli, A. (2015). *Contemporary cosmopolitanism.* London: Bloomsbury Academic.

Thörn, H. (2009). *Anti-Apartheid and the emergence of a global civil society.* Basingstoke: Palgrave Macmillan.

Turner, B. S. (2002). Cosmopolitan virtue, globalization and patriotism'. *Theory, Culture & Society* 19(1-2): 45-63.

Vernon, R. (2010). *Cosmopolitan regard: political membership and global justice.* New York: Cambridge University Press.

Volkmer, I. (2014). *The global public sphere: public communication in the age of reflective interdependence.* Cambridge: Polity Press.

Walker, J. W. St. G., & Thompson, A. S. (eds.) (2008). *Critical mass: the emergence of global civil society.* Waterloo, CA: Wilfrid Laurier University Press.

Chapter 6

Talk to me and I will talk for you: Relationships between Citizens and Politics on the example of Portuguese Members of Parliament online communication

Evandro Oliveira and Gisela Gonçalves

Introduction

As digital communication technologies started to develop, a new environment for communication was formed. What was initially considered just a roll-out of innovations soon took the form of the World Wide Web, laying the groundwork for the emergence of Web 2.0. What could be called Digital Evolution took on its own *milieu* and setting (Macnamara, 2010, Breakenridge, 2008).

Characterized by the easy creation and exchange of User Generated Content (Kaplan & Haenlein, 2010: 61), social media creates new circumstances and possibilities for public discussions. With it comes a new stage for the public sphere, which creates blurred borders with the public space. Furthermore, social media also means, due to its communications conditions and routines, that there is a clear separation of time and space and even a change in the linear understanding of the communication sequence and flow. Social media not only complements traditional media but has specific characteristics such as mobility, complexity, plurality of channels and actors, interactivity, network structures, and constant change.

From a social theory perspective, social media and modern online communication can be framed by the dominance of abstract systems and the characteristics of modernity defined by Giddens (1991). Because of the process of "disembedding", social relations are removed from local contexts of interaction, creating new contexts. Those interactions become more and more mediated by new technical interfaces, and are often based on trust in the "correctness of abstract principles (technical knowledge)" (Giddens 1991: p. 34). Those changes add an extra challenge to social action and relations.

Politicians all over Europe have quickly taken to this virtual space. Since 2011, an average of 70% of Members of the European Parliament (MEPs) regularly communicate with citizens via social media. Since 2011, the European Parliament has also had a mobile version of the website with an integrated Facebook page that disseminates content from the MEPs' presence on their own online platforms, including Twitter, blogs and the EP's official website (EP, 2011). Parliamentarians' websites offer a range of Web 1.0 and Web 2.0 features and strive to stimulate engaging and interactive experiences (Lilleker, 2011). But, not limited to informal discussion, in 2012, the European Commission performed a public online consultation, in which European citizens could express their opinions about their rights (Andrecs, 2011).[1] According to the 2015 European Parliament Digital Trends Survey (EPDTS), the European Parliament currently has 572 of 751 MEPs (76%) on its list of those with Twitter accounts and 663 MEPs (88%) on its list of Facebook users.[2] Learning about breaking news, engaging with people through dialogue and expressing their views to stakeholders are the main reasons why MEPs become involved in social media (EPDTS, 2015).

Contrary to other European countries, few studies have focused attention on MPs' online communication practices in Portugal.[3] A previous study came to the conclusion that three main obstacles existed to the development of a "digital democracy" in Portugal: the predominance of television in the media system, a political parliamentary system that does not promote direct contact with citizens, and the existence of unmotivated citizens (Cardoso, Cunha & Nascimento, 2003). This study also showed that only 5.1% of MPs frequently used personal websites, 2.6% used newsgroups and 1.3% used chat rooms to do their parliamentary work. Has this reality changed over these last 10 years with the new evolutions of the digital era and the spread of mobile media?

[1] http://europedecides.eu/2014/06/the-new-european-parliament-on-twitter-look-whos-talking/

[2] http://www.epdigitaltrends.eu/assets/ep-digital-trends-survey_full_results.pdf

[3] See, for example, regarding the UK's situation, Jackson and Lilleker, 2004; or Lusoli, Ward, and Gibson, 2006.

Another more recent exploratory study was conducted about the use of Web 2.0 tools on the Portuguese Parliament's website that aim to increase interaction between Members of Parliament and citizens – forums, blogs, petitions – and revealed a small degree of participation by both parties (Serra, 2012). This study agrees with the findings by Leston-Bandeira (2012) about petitions as a participatory tool:

> What may be lacking is the development of more participative citizens, though data on petitions shows that the Portuguese have learned how to make use of this constitutional right (p.399).

In line with the "relationship management" theory, which claims that in order for an organization to be successful it needs to put effort into establishing and nurturing relationships with its publics and balance mutual interests (Ledingham, 2006, 2011), the main goal of this chapter is to analyse whether or not online communication tools stimulate citizen-politician relationships. In particular, we aim to find out and reflect on how social media is being used to foster interaction and dialogue between citizens and Members of Parliament, specifically at the Portuguese Parliament – *Assembleia da República.* Our main focus is on this relationship, considering the representative democratic principles that work towards public dialogic needs in a framework of legitimization and transparency, and isolating it from structures and interactions on the platforms made available centrally by the political party or by the Parliament. This approach includes the sociological framework laid down by Giddens in his structuration theory (1984). Furthermore, the dialogical paradigm and maturity in social media communication is considered in the sense of a "transformative discussion", meaning authentic and open communication that produces a means of changing an opinion or perspective. It occurs when stakeholders lose their position of power by engaging in an authentic and open dialogic exchange in the Habermasian sense but applied to online communication (see Oliveira & Winchenbach, 2011).

Literature review

The literature review is divided into two sections: the first is a reflection on the sociological context of social media communication, and the second focuses on its relationship with online political communication and relationship management studies from a political public relations perspective.

Social Media Communication

Over the last years, the growth in the number of mobile devices and the improvement in connectivity, like LTE systems[4] and others, support the trend that technologically mediated communication has reached diverse sociodemographic groups (van Eimeren & Frees, 2012: 362; PEW Research, 2012: 5-6). While in its initial phase only the young could be included in social media communication, now the "digital natives" are only one group of users.

The emancipation of stakeholders and publics demands and pushes for a shift away from hierarchical structures to produce, demand and perform a form of interaction and communication that is more democratic in its principles (Brown 2009: 2; Coombs 1998: 289; Sweetser 2010). This is a consequence of an authoritative competence developed by structural usability. Publishing is easier and dependent on access rather than personal capacity. In that process, the perception of users changes from passive recipients to investigative multipliers (Zerfaß, 2007: 41). Furthermore, social aspects such as authenticity gain importance and there is a shift from general groups to communities, dissolving authoritative competences. In line with that, the traditional information flow through broadcasting in mass media is replaced or complemented by the selection and sharing of specific information in a new form of gatekeeping. This coincides, in turn, with new open forms of persuasion.

Besides structures and technical possibilities, as well as access to those tools, what O'Reilly (2005) considers a *societal paradigm shift* is becoming stronger and bolder. This shift is considered to be due to the fact that changes in societal exchange and interaction are happening in basic manners and principles. Schmidt (2008: 34-35) makes an analogy of three particularly relevant issues of change

[4] LTE stands for Long-Term Evolution and is also known as 4G. It is a standard for high-speed data for mobile phones, data terminals and wireless communication.

and connects them with levels of society. At micro level, the boundaries between private and public are dissolving as simple publication possibilities facilitate a rise in a variety of "personal publics". At meso level, new technologies demand specific media literacy. Different levels of media literacy are creating "digital gaps". At macro level, established and implemented concepts and practices of communication management are not ready to deal with the quantity and modern forms of collaboration and participation.

Levine *et al.* (2009) describe those characteristics in the context of what they call the Cluetrain Manifesto, in which those changes are described and systematized – especially the imperative for dialogue, which is seen as the willingness and openness to talk to the public. Pleil (2007: 18) (See Table 6.1) breaks down the chronological development of online communication based on what is defined by the "internet galaxy" and the "Google world".

In this case, social media communication characteristics set the tone for users' roles and demands, as well as the main communication aim and role of online PR. Whilst in digital and internet PR communication is monological and users are seen as recipients with options for action, in Cluetrain PR the dialogical and network-oriented characteristics demand an understanding of the users as communication partners and not only recipients. This is true in that the communication aims to argue with and understand publics rather than inform and persuade them.

As we will discuss ahead, political communication according to this understanding poses many challenges that turn out to be more time-consuming and costly than traditional, unidirectional information dissemination. Moreover, the structures and processes are more complex and demand greater professionalization and skills. In a nutshell, the new online platforms cannot just be seen as an additional technological enabler, but instead they produce a *thorough shift* in "the way it's being used" (Pavlik, 2007: 9).

Online political communication and relationship management

Democratic societies are experiencing a democratic deficit largely visible in the increased abstention in political elections and general disenchantment with politics. This deficit is, to a large extent, a cri-

Characteristics	Types of Online PR		
	Digital PR	Internet PR	Cluetrain PR
Environment	Internet Galaxy		Google World
Communication	monological	monological (indirect feedback)	dialogical, network oriented
Users' Role	recipients	recipients with limited action options	communication partners organized in a network
Demands	PR competences, understanding of hypermediality	Content Management, social research	strategic and interpersonal skills; special position of trust;
Expenditure	relatively small,	high technical effort Need for their own site (s) for online PR	very time-consuming; continuous task ("always on")
Role of Online PR	executive	channelling	openness, empowerment of stakeholders
Main Aim	information	persuasion	understanding, argumentation

Table 6.1: Comparison of the three types of online PR (Source: modified from Pleil, 2007: 18)

sis of trust in traditional political parties and government, according to which citizens feel misrepresented and hence alienated from rightful participation in their political destiny.

It is no wonder, therefore, that since the mid-1990s the rise and spread of the internet has been observed as the solution to the illnesses of democracy, enabling "the virtual community" (Rheingold, 1993), "virtual democracy" (Scheer, 1994), and radical new ways of living (Dertouzos, 1997). In fact, ever since the internet became part of the politician's toolkit, and especially with the development of Web 2.0, more attention has been paid to new opportunities for politician-voter interaction, as demonstrated by the much publicized 2008 Obama campaign, known as "the first internet election".

However, and despite it being a debated issue, there is no consensus regarding new media's potential to increase citizens' political engagement and participation. Earlier studies, albeit to different degrees, have suggested a positive or optimistic perspective of the internet's role in enhancing political trust, pluralism and widening citizen participation in governmental processes (e.g., Chadwick 2006; Curtice & Norris, 2004; Norris, 2003; Rheinghold, 1993) and have stressed its importance for "horizontal communication", which is central to civic interaction (Dahlgren, 2005). In general, these studies have underlined how digitally mediated direct representation could provide the basis for more dialogical and deliberative democracy instead of the "dialogue of the deaf which tends to characterize contemporary political representation" (Coleman, 2005: 177).

Nevertheless, more empirically focused research has, contrariwise, shown a more negative, pessimistic, sceptical approach, pointing to what is often referred to as the "normalization thesis": politics on the internet is nothing more than "politics as usual", dominated by the traditional, offline players (Margolis & Resnick, 2000; Larsson, 2013; Schweitzer, 2008, 2011).

Over time, as presented in Table 6.2, these positive/negative approaches have led researchers to adopt one or more dichotomies when interpreting their findings in online political communication (see Larsson and Svensson, 2014, for a comprehensive overview). One cannot help wonder if this dichotomization is a not a dead end. Some researchers, indeed, have already suggested a third, middle-ground alternative when studying the politicians' online activities. Jackson and Lilleker (2009), for example, suggest a hybrid, midway between innovation and stagnation, as a description of what political parties are doing online. In their analysis they found that British political parties have sought to experiment with Web 2.0 applications and appear to be using some aspects of the technology but not others. They found that they have sought to create a "Web 1.5" that offers the advantages of both Web 1.0 (control and content dissemination) and Web 2.0 (interactivity).

The on-going discussion about the merits of online communication potential can also be easily found in the political public relations (PPR) literature, especially literature grounded in the relationship management paradigm. It was Stromback & Kiousis (2011)

(More) positive	**(More) negative**	**Authors (examples)**
Equalization/ innovation	Normalization	Gibson *et al.*, 2008; Lilleker *et al.*, 2011; Margolis and Resnick, 2000; Schweitzer, 2008, 2011
Optimistic	Pessimistic	Coleman and Blumler, 2009
Cyber-optimist	Cyber-realist	Shane, 2004; Wright, 2012
Optimist	Sceptic	Christensen and Bengtsson, 2001

Table 6.2: Dichotomized approaches to online politics (Source: adapted from Larsson and Svensson, 2014: 3)

who, with the intention of bridging the gap between public relations and political communication theory, brought the relationship management perspective into the definition of PPR:

> Political public relations is the management process by which an organization or individual actor for political purposes, through purposeful communication and action, seeks to influence and to establish, build, and maintain *beneficial relationships* [emphasis added] and reputations with its key publics to help support its mission and achieve its goals. (Stromback & Kiousis, 2011, p.8)

In the light of relationship management theory, *beneficial relationships* would be characterized by mutual positive interdependence. To better understand this interdependence, Ledingham and Bruning (1998), key authors in the development of relationship management theory, identified five dimensions of organization-public relationships that influence publics' perception of their relationship with an organization: trust, openness, involvement, commitment and investment in the relationship. Moreover, the authors found that better perception of these aspects correlates with more favourable dispositions toward an organization. *Trust* describes the feeling that those in the relationship can rely on each other. *Openness* refers to being engaged in communication in a frank way. Involvement means that both the organization and public are committed to furthering each other's interests and thus maintain a long-term relationship. *Investment* "refers to the time, energy, feelings, efforts and other resources given to building the relationship" (Ledingham & Bruning, 1998, p. 58).

It is worth mentioning that relationship management research has had a strong boost due to the internet's potential to increase dialogic communication between organizations and their publics (Jo & Kim, 2003; McAllister-Spooner, 2009). Dialogue is "any negotiated exchange of ideas and opinions" (Kent & Taylor, 1998, p. 325) and represents the efforts made by those involved in a relationship to participate in an open and honest exchange. The dialogic theory argues that in order for a good relationship to exist there must be ethical and high-quality dialogue between the organization and the publics (Kent & Taylor, 1998; 2002). Organizations must be open to this conversation because dialogue contributes to developing symmetrical relationships (Kent & Taylor, 1998).

The public relations relational perspective could provide a theoretical basis for understanding the construction of the citizen-political actor relationship. As Taylor and Kent (2004) stated: "The Internet and the WWW can theoretically improve relationships between elected officials and their constituents" (p. 60). However, despite being a well-explored topic in public relations literature, scholarship has focused less on the political organization-citizen relationships (Karlsson *et al.*, 2013; Levenshus, 2010; Seltzer *et al.*, 2013; Seltzer & Zhang, 2011; Sweetser & Tedesco, 2014). Moreover, research in that field mainly focuses on the role of websites and web-based communication during electoral campaigns and influence on voters' party loyalty. Levenshus (2010), for example, used a relational approach to study President Obama's use of social media in his 2008 presidential campaign by analysing the Obama website and its news articles and by interviewing campaign staff. Her findings indicate that social media was primarily used for building and maintaining relationships between the President and his constituents.

This and other studies are based on the assumption that social media communications foster dialogue, and that these can lead to relationship building (see, for example, Sweetser, 2011). Bearing in mind the potential but also the pitfalls of social media in public relations (Duhé, 2012), in this chapter we aim to contribute to the ongoing debate using the example of Portuguese Members of Parliaments' online communication. With the cross analysis and discussion of the results, we hope to offer a reality check on the Portuguese context and add to our knowledge about this communication context.

Method[5]

Based on the literature review, three research questions were established to guide data collection and analysis:

> RQ1 – What are the Portuguese parliamentary political groups' rules, governance structures and platforms?
> RQ2 – Which channels are used by Portuguese MPs?
> RQ3 – How do Portuguese MPs communicate online?

A multimethod approach was designed to study how social media is being used to foster interaction and dialogue between citizens and Members of Parliament. We analyse the rules and resources as a structure, and we also analyse the interaction. The dynamics are considered according to Anthony Giddens' Structuration Theory (1984) approach. Firstly, we mapped the channels used by Portuguese MPs and, at the same time, we identified rules, governance structures and platforms maintained by the political parties and by the Parliament. Contact was made by phone and email to ask the communication manager questions and posts were simulated to see reactions and handling methods.

In order to implement the analysis, six dimensions were identified that translate the main aspects highlighted in the theoretical framework, as well as central questions in the communication management field: i) Centralization of communication activities; ii) strategic and integrated approach to communication management, iii) presence of dialogic approach, iv) interaction in the form of answers to questions and posts; v) Censorship of content (deleted content); vi) Social media governance, which was operationalized as a list of the following 12 items: participative corporate culture; commitment of top management; human resources; person in charge of social media in each department; monitoring tools; social media workshops; seminars and training; social media guidelines; strategy papers; key performance indicators for measuring success; spe-

[5] We want to thank the 2013-2014 Strategic Communication Master's students from the University of Beira Interior (UBI) for the help in collecting online data.

cific budget; software and hardware; a dedicated social media department (according to Fink *et al.*, 2011); and personified communication, meaning the disclosure of the identity of the person posting the content, either his/her name or function.

Simultaneously, a content analysis of Facebook and Twitter interactions over a period of two months (March and April 2014) was performed in order to understand how the MPs interact with the public and what kind of dialogue can be found on the social media channel. This was classified into one of eight categories in order to describe the reality of that communication in terms of intensity, intention and approach. The dimensions proposed by Pleil (2007: 18) were also taken into consideration as the main aim of communication acts in each dimension to distinguish between online PR and Google PR (previously discussed in the literature review section, Table 6.1). They include: the mix of channels used by active MPs (1); the number of posts on Twitter and Facebook (2), which were divided into personal and political/public posts (3); the main communication aim(s) of that content (information, persuasion or argumentation) (4); the mean average of likes per post (5); the average number of comments per post (6); the average number of shares per post (6), if there was interaction in the form of discourse (7); and what web architecture was used by the MPs.[6]

The analysis was performed for all six Portuguese parties that have parliamentary representation in the 12th legislature:

- CDS/PP – Democratic Social Centre/Popular Party (Christian democrats, office-seeking)
- PPD/PSD – Social Democratic Party (government, catch-all party)
- PS – Socialist Party (opposition, catch-all party)
- PCP – Portuguese Communist Party (Marxist, ideological party)
- BE – Left Bloc (Marxist, ideological party)
- PEV – Green party

[6] The architecture of the web is the way that the content and flow are organized in and across several channels and tools (see Oliveira & Winchenbach, 2011: 20).

Results and Discussion

In terms of structures, all the different parliamentary groups are active on the web or at least have a presence with a centralized form of communication for all online communications. There is no room for politicians to participate in the party channels and structures other then through a single dissemination upon request. In terms of online communication, we provide an overview of the parties according to the categories established in Table 6.3. Some of this information was collected during phone and email contact with parties' communication managers.

Group	MPs	Centr.	Strategic/ Integrated	Dialogic	Answer	Censur.	Govern.	Pers.
PPD/PSD	108	YES	NO	NO	NO	YES	NO	NO
PS	74	YES	YES	NO	NO	NO	NO	NO
CDS-PP	24	YES	NO	NO	NO	NO	NO	NO
PCP	14	YES	NO	NO	NO	YES	NO	NO
BE	8	YES	YES	NO	NO	NO	NO	NO
PEV	2	YES	NO	NO	YES	NO	NO	NO

Table 6.3: Analysis overview of the parties' online communication

None of the parties have a dialogical approach, any governance items or personalized communication. It is very surprising that the largest group (PPD-PSD) performs censorship, as well as the communist party. Only the smallest group (PEV) replies online. All of the groups have centralized communication, but we only see signs of a strategic and integrated approach to communication management in two of them.

In the second stage of this research, the parliamentary groups' specific channels and communication activities were examined. After immersion, the main and outstanding elements were collected and can be seen in Table 6.4.

GRUPO PARLAMENTAR PARTIDO SOCIAL DEMOCRATA PSD	• Active since 2009 with dedicated MP group tools • Website; FB, Sapo Vídeos, Flickr and YouTube • Twitter has not been used since 2011 • There are no regular updates of the website • There is no interaction • Comments are often deleted or hidden • Content is not tailored • FB content analysis: low posting frequency (just 21 posts in 2 months)
Grupo Parlamentar PARTIDO SOCIALISTA	• Integration of social media tools in the last 5 years • Strategic use of information • Dedicated website Tab; FB, Twitter, G+, Flickr, YouTube, RSS • Intensive and organized publication (e.g. YouTube) • There is no interaction • Comments are not deleted • Content is partly tailored • FB content analysis: mostly informative posts, always with images of MPs

CDS PP Grupo Parlamentar	• Active since 2011 • Website; Facebook, Twitter, YouTube • Strong political agenda • Flickr was used from 2008-2010 • Standalone video content • Publishing of news content from the media • Controlled by one communication manager • FB – link to the FB page of the political party leader
PCP	• Website with information • YouTube but not used as social media • No interaction desired
PEV osverdes.pt	• Active since end of 2011 • No dedicated channels for MPs • Website; Facebook, Twitter, YouTube • Strong political and ideological agenda • Answers to posts • No content discussion • Partially adapted content

Bloco de Esquerda	• Website with detailed, organized information • Website, Facebook, YouTube, Flickr, (not updated – MySpace, Twitter, Hi5) • No rules but performed by Com. Dep. • FB is used to spread content (partially automatic)

Table 6.4: Analysis of the parliamentary groups' online communication

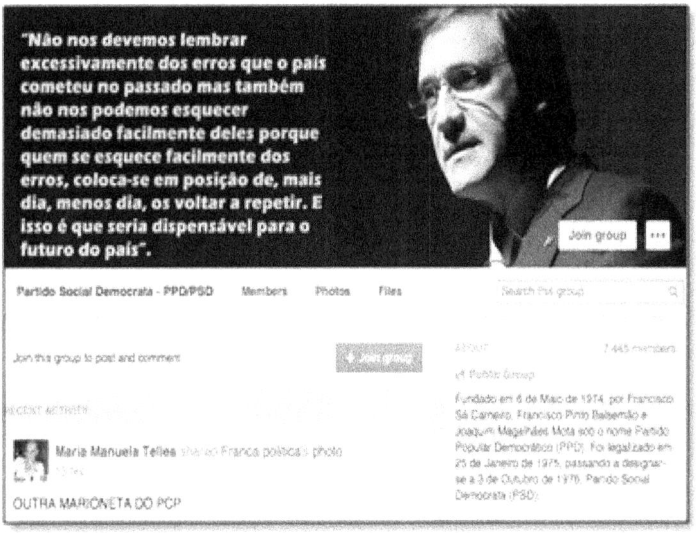

Figure 6.1: Screeenshot with the unofficial Facebook group of the largest parliamentary group in Portugal.

Four groups have channels dedicated to the parliamentary group (PSD, PS, CDS-PP and BE). The BE has merged everything into a central website, with a dedicated page for the parliamentary group, while its Facebook page is just used to spread content, mostly videos. Despite the existence of those channels for exchanges and democratic political debate, we notice that little discussion happens on those forums. On a Facebook search, we found alternative spaces – none of which were official – that offered the possibility for discussion and exchanges of different views. These Facebook groups had many more followers than the official ones and interaction was very intense (see Figure 6.1). These results allow us to have an insight to answer RQ1 – *What are the Portuguese parliamentary political groups' rules, governance structures and platforms?*

Mapping parliamentary online communication

At the third stage, we look into the structures, resources and processes organized and promoted by the Parliament, to outline some insights to address RQ2 – *Which channels are used by Portuguese MPs?*

We noticed that a great deal of effort was put into online communication at an early stage but they were mostly technical efforts to enable and stimulate MPs' online presence. The Parliament has a website and official tools; it offers political groups and MPs the opportunity to activate their own page, blog and link to social media. Nevertheless, as we can see in Table 6.5, only a few members of the Portuguese parliamentary groups have created a personal page there, and only 4 use the blogroll device.

The scenario gets even worse when taking into account that the blogs were last updated in 2012. Looking more closely at MPs' personal pages, there are only 4 but they are not updated, and only one of this group of MPs is still an MP today; the others no longer have that role. This clearly shows a decrease in MPs' interest in using personal pages compared with the 2003 study (Cardoso *et al*, 2003), which found that 5,1% of MPs – 15 – frequently used personal websites.

Group	MPs	Personal page Parlamento.pt	FB	Other
PPD/PSD	108	4	2 A; 1 NA	Twitter: 1A YouTube: 1A
PS	74	8	6 A; 1 NA	Twitter: 1A; 1 NA YouTube: 2 A Instagram: 1 A Blogs: 2 A; 2 NA
BE	8	4	2 A	0
CDS-PP	24	0	-	-
PCP	14	0	-	-
PEV	2	0	-	-

Table 6.5: Overview of the tools provided by the Parliament and other social media tools used by MPs as individuals

Content analysis

In order to have a close look and more in-depth understanding of the relationship between citizens and MPs and answer RQ3 – *How do Portuguese MPs communicate online?* – a two-month analysis (March-April 2014) of MPs' activities on social media was performed to obtain a picture of how social media is being used by Portuguese politicians in an effort to take a broad, empirical approach to the topics of research.

In total, 730 posts from 17 accounts, operated by 10 MPs, were collected and analysed. We can see that less than 10 per cent of MPs engage in online communication with citizens. They represent only three of the six parliamentary groups (PSD – 2; PS – 6 and BE 2). Furthermore, more than the half of the active MPs are from one parliamentary group and they were in the opposition party.

The two main platforms that were used for online communication were Facebook (57%) and Twitter (26%). Blogs, YouTube and Instagram were also used but much more rarely. (see Figure 6.2).

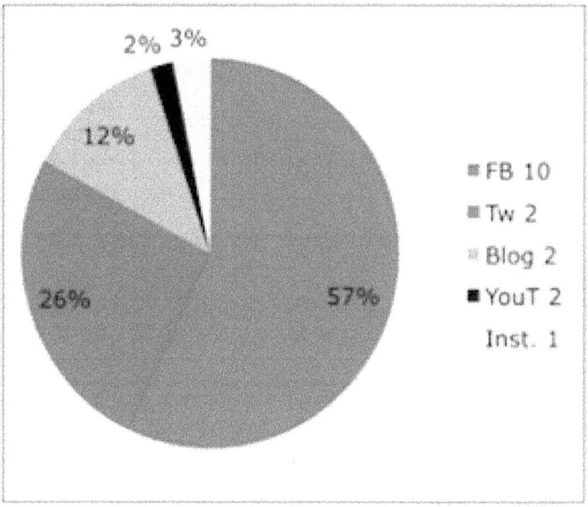

Figure 6.2: Online communication posts

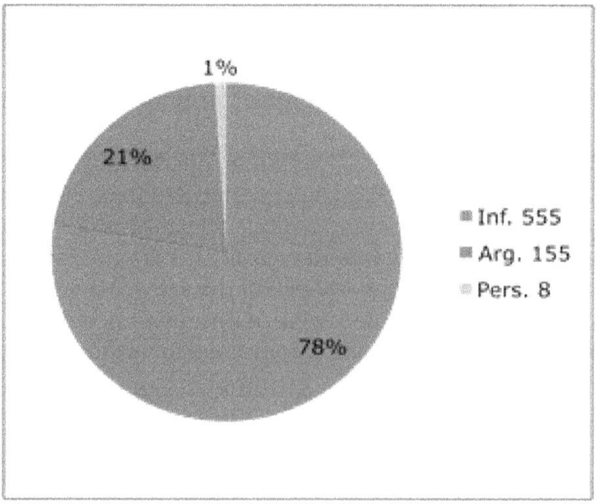

n=730 posts on social networks by Portuguese MPs in March and April 2014. Divided into Informative, Argumentative and Persuasive

Figure 6.3: Communication main aim in online communication content

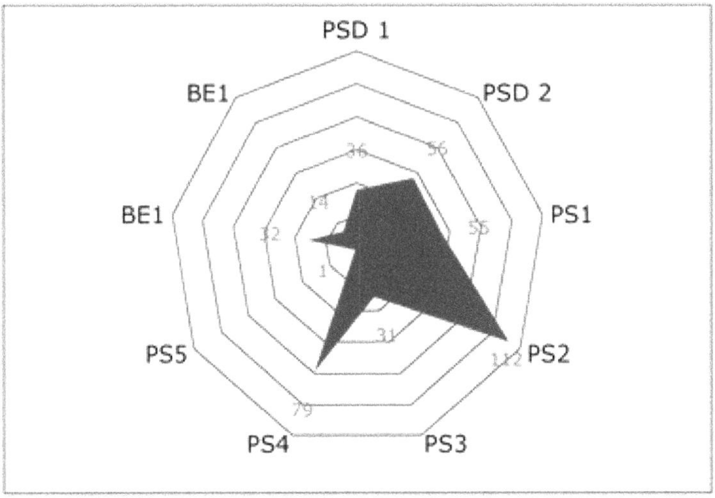

n=417 posts on FB by Portuguese MPs in March and April 2014. MPs n=10

Figure 6.4: Posts on Facebook per MP

In regard to the communication aim of the post (see Figure 6.3), almost eight in every ten posts (78%) were informative, one in every 5 (21%) was argumentative and only one per cent showed persuasive objectives. We recall here that informative and persuasive communication is not seen as dialogic, but rather as a monologic approach as defined in the literature review.

When we look closer at interactions on Facebook, we notice that in total 417 posts were made by 10 MPs (see Figure 6.4). There are two MPs from the PS group who produced 191 posts, equivalent to over 45 per cent of them. If we exclude the two MPs who only published one post each, we have an average posting of one post every two days from the others. That means that six of them are quite active in terms of publication numbers, while two are extremely active (more than one publication per day) and two are almost inactive, with one post per day.

When we look at the character of the posts (see Table 6.1 and Figure 6.5), it can be seen that MPs use social media to post more about political rather than personal issues. However, we can see an inversion of this trend by one member of the opposition party: the PS.

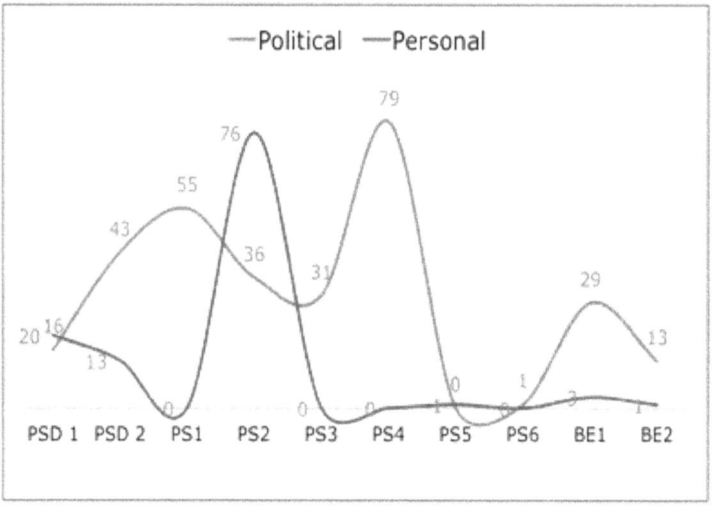

n=417 posts on FB by Portuguese MPs in March and April 2014. MPs n=10

Figure 6.5: Posts on Facebook per MP divided into two categories

In total, seven out of ten public posts had political content and three had personal content. On the other side, we see that two MPs posted more than one third of the content. Those MPs have no public personal posts (see Table 6.6).

On average, most of the MPs have a quite low average number of comments: no more than 8. Only one has 103 comments per post on average. In regard to visitors' activities on MPs' Facebook profiles, they clearly choose to "Like" specific content but few "Comment" on the posts. This tendency provides information regarding the interaction and relationship and the use of those platforms and channels to really engage in discussion or not. We see that not only is the quantity is very small, but the quality and depth are limited as well.

	Political	**Personal**
PSD 1	16	20
PSD 2	43	13
PS1	55	0
PS2	36	76
PS3	31	0
PS4	79	0
PS5	0	1
PS6	1	0
BE1	29	3
BE2	13	1
	303	114
	73%	27%

Table 6.6: Overview of the posts by MP, classified into Political and Personal focus.n = 417 posts on FB by Portuguese MPs in March and April 2014. MPs n= 10

	Likes	**Comments**	**Share**
PSD1	45.33	3.58	0.88
PSD2	56.23	4.2	1.2
PS1	670	103.03	81.76
PS2	35	7.64	1.36
PS3	15	0.58	0.74
PS4	11	8	0
PS5	29	1.18	1.13
PS6	6	0	0
BE1	65	3.68	23.12
BE2	31	2.28	7.93

Table 6.7: Overview of FB interactions by MP.

Conclusion

With this research, we aimed to understand how online communication tools stimulate citizen-politics relationship management. In particular, we reflect on how social media is being used to foster interaction and dialogue between citizens and the members of the Portuguese parliament. Research was divided into two main areas of inquiry. The channels used by Portuguese MPs were mapped and, at the same time, the rules, governance structures and platforms maintained by the parliamentary groups and by the Parliament were identified. The MP-citizen interaction routines were depicted, particularly as regards social media.

All the different parliamentary groups have a presence on the web through dedicated channels, blogs, their own pages or links to social media. The analysis has revealed that there is minimal, ad-hoc use of social media, which means that the professionalization of MPs' online communication is low. That is, we can observe inverse institutionalization dynamics and low professionalization. This means that at an earlier stage, many channels and systems were created but they are decreasingly used by the MPs. This confirms what was found by other studies that looked into professionalization in other Portuguese organizations (See Linke & Oliveira 2015). Also, parties' governance of social media is barely put into practice at all. The visible results of "structuration", in Giddens' sense, do not take into account this particular angle of communication management. We can see that on one side there is a centralized, non-strategic use of online communication, while on the other, the handling by those involved, especially the MPs, was not enough to be addressed centrally.

The main findings indicate a very weak use of the web's potential for relationship-building between politicians and citizens. This has been also found in other research contexts in the Portuguese political realm (see Serra & Gonçalves, 2015). Providing information is a predominant function over promoting interaction in the use of internet communication. As the data has shown, for example, only 10% of the MPs are active on Facebook, with informative (monologic) posts, and there is a very low average of comments per post (8%). Visitors opt for using the "Like" feature and rarely "Comment" on the content of the posts.

These findings suggest that the internet's dialogical promise has not yet materialized in the Portuguese parliamentary realm. Of 230 MPs, only 10 are very active on Facebook, and the new medium is being used merely to disseminate information, not to promote interaction and much less dialogue. Furthermore, we may even conclude that by allowing users to comment on posts on Facebook, MPs appear to be interested in communicating with citizens in an online public space. However, a citizen-politician relationship cannot flourish where there is censorship of political debate. That is, when content that is less favourable to the political party's objectives are simply deleted, as highlighted in the discussion section on findings.

When we compare the fact that 5 per cent of MPs are active in this field, compared with the average of 70 per cent of the Members of the European Parliament (MEPs) who communicate regularly with citizens via social media, we see that Portugal trails far behind Europe regarding this issue.

Nevertheless, and interestingly enough, the data also shows that political discussion takes place in spontaneous online spaces: on closed Facebook groups. Despite the obvious limitations of our study, in particular due to the restricted frame of analysis of two months and the complex and multimethod approach that provides exploratory rather than conclusive insights, we hope to have opened new avenues of inquiry into contemporary political communication from both citizens' and politicians' perspectives.

Bibliography

Andrecs, R (2011). Die nutzung des web 2.0 durch die EU-Instituitionen. In F. Setzen (Hrsg) *Europapolitische kommunikation und web 2.0: formen, trends, herausforderungen und chancen.* Förderverein Europa Zentrum Baden-Württemberg.

Breakenridge, D. (2008). *PR 2.0: new media, new tools, new audiences.* Upper Saddle River, NJ: FT Press.

Brown, R. (2009). *Public relations and the social web: how to use social media and web 2.0 in communications.* London: Kogan Page.

Cardoso, G., Cunha, C. & Nascimento, S. (2003). O parlamento português na construção de uma democracia digital. *Sociologia, Problemas e Práticas,* 42: 113-140.

Chadwick, A. (2006). *Internet politics: states, citizens, and new communication technologies.* New York: Oxford University Press.

Christensen, H.S. & Bengtsson, Å. (2001). The political competence of internet participants: evidence from Finland. *Information, Communication & Society,* 14(6): 896-916.

Coleman, S. (2005). New mediation and direct representation: reconceptualizing representation in the digital age. *New Media & Society,* 7(2): 177-198.

Coleman, S. & Blumler, J.G. (2009). *The internet and democratic citizenship: theory, practice and policy.* Cambridge: Cambridge University Press.

Coombs, W. T. (1998). The internet as potential equalizer: new leverage for confronting social irresponsibility. *Public Relations Review,* 24(3): 289-303.

Curtice, J. & Norris, P. (2004). 'e-politics'? The impact of the internet on political trust and participation. In A. Park; J. Curtice; K. Thomson; C. Bromley & M. Philips (Eds.) (2004). *British social attitudes: the 21st report,* (pp. 99-118). London: Sage.

Dahlgren, P. (2005). The internet, public spheres, and political communication: dispersion and deliberation. *Political Communication,* 22 (2): 147-162.

Dertouzos, M. L. (1997). *What will be: how the new world of information will change our lives.* New York: Harperedge.

Duhé, S. (2012). A thematic analysis of 30 years of public relations literature addressing the potential and pitfalls of new media. In Duhé, S. (Ed.), *New media and public relations* (2. ed., pp. 1-2). New York: Peter Lang.

EPDTS (2015). European parliament digital trends survey, fleishmanhillard survey, available at: `http://www.epdigitaltrends.eu/assets/ep-digital-trends-survey_full_results.pdf`

Fink, S., Zerfass, A. & Linke, A. (2011). Social media governance 2011: kompetenzen, strukturen und strategien von unternehmen, behörden und non-profit-organisationen für die online-kommunikation im social web: ergebnisse einer empirischen studie bei kommunikationsverantwortlichen. Leipzig & Wiesbaden: Universität Leipzig & FFPR.

Gibson, R.K.; Lusoli, W. & Ward, S. (2008). Nationalizing and normalizing the local? A comparative analysis of online candidate campaigning in Australia and Britain. *Journal of Information Technology & Politics,* 4(4), 15-30.

Giddens, A. (1991). *The consequences of modernity* (1st paperback ed.). Cambridge: Polity Press.

Giddens, A. (1984). *The constitution of society: outline of the theory of structuration.* Cambridge: Polity Press.

Gonçalves, G. & Serra, J. P. (2015). Online relationship management and digital participation in the political sphere: a communicative myth?. In A. D. Melo, I. Somerville & G. Gonçalves, *Organisational and strategic communication research: european perspectives II* (pp. 9-26), CECS, UM: Braga.

Jackson, N.A. & Lilleker, D. G. (2009). Building an architecture of participation? Political parties and web 2.0 in Britain. *Journal of Information Technology & Politics*, 6 (3-4): 232-250.

Jo, S., & Kim, Y. (2003). The effect of web characteristics on relationship building. *Journal of Public Relations Research*, 158(3): 199-223.

Kaplan, A. M., & Haenlein, M. (2010). Users of the world, unite! The challenges and opportunities of social media. *Business Horizons*, 53(1): 59-68.

Karlsson, M., Clerwall, C., & Buskvist, U. (2013). Political public relations on the net: a relationship management perspective. *Public Relations Journal*, 7 (4).

Kent, M. L. & Taylor, M. (1998). Building dialogic relationships through the world wide web. *Public Relations Review*, 24 (3): 321-334.

Kent, M. L. & Taylor, M. (2002). Toward a dialogic theory of public relations. *Public Relations Review*, 28 (1): 21-37.

Larsson, A. O. (2013). 'Rejected bits of program code': why notions of 'politics 2.0' remain (mostly) unfulfilled. *Journal of Information Technology & Politics*, 10(1), 72-85.

Larsson, A. O. & Svensson, J. (2014). Politicians online: identifying current research opportunities. *First Monday*, volume 19, number 4.

Ledingham, J. A. (2006). Relationship management: a general theory of public relations. In C. H. Botan & V. Hazleton (Eds.), *Public relations theory II* (pp.465-483). Lawrence Erlbaum Associates, Mahwah, NJ.

Ledingham, J. A. (2011). Political public relations and relationship management. In J. Stromback & S. Kiousis (Ed.), *Political public relations* (pp.235-253). New York: Routledge.

Ledingham, J. A. & Bruning, S. D. (1998). Relationship management and public relations: dimensions of organization-public relationship. *Public Relations Review*, 24 (1): 55-65.

Leston-Bandeira, C. & Tibúrcio, T. (2012). Developing links despite the parties: parliament and citizens in Portugal. *The Journal of Legislative Studies*, 18 (3-4): 384-402.

Levenshus, A. (2010). Online relationship management in a presidential campaign: a case study of the Obama campaign's management of its internet-integrated grassroots efforts. *Journal of Public Relations Research*, 22(3): 313-335.

Levine, R.; Locke, C.; Searls, D. & Weinberger, D. (2009). The Cluetrain manifesto. In R. Levine, C. Locke, D. Searls, & D. Weinberger (Eds.), The Cluetrain manifesto (10. ed., pp. xiii-xx). New York: Basic Books.

Lilleker, D & Michalska, K. (2011). MEPs online: understanding communication strategies for remote representatives. Paper presented at the *European Consortium of Political Researchers Conference*, Reykjavik (Iceland), September 2011. Retrieved from `http://eprints.bournemouth.ac.uk/21106/3/Lilleker.MEPs.pdf` on 22.08.2014

Linke, A. & Oliveira, E. (2015) Quantity or quality? The professionalization of social media communication in Portugal and Germany: a comparison. *Public Relations Review*, 41 (2): 305-307.

Lusoli, W.; Ward, S. & Gibson, R. (2006) (Re)connecting politics? Parliament, the public and the internet. *Parliamentary Affairs*, 59 (1): 24-42.

Macnamara, J. (2010). Public relations and the social: how practitioners are using, or abusing, social media. *Asia Pacific Public Relations Journal, 11*(1): 21-39.

Macnamara, J. & Zerfass, A. (2012). Social media communication in organisations: the challenges of balancing openness, strategy and management. *International Journal of Strategic Communication*, 6(4): 287-308.

McAllister-Spooner, S. (2009). Fulfilling the dialogic promise: a ten-year reflective survey on dialogic Internet principles. *Public Relations Review*, 39 (2): 320-222.

Margolis, M. & Resnick, D. (2000). *Politics as usual: the cyberspace "revolution"*. London: Sage.

Norris, P. (2003). Preaching to the converted? Pluralism, participation and party websites. *Party Politics*, 1(1): 21-45.

Oliveira, E. & Winchenbach, U. (2011) Social media: relevante plattformen, answendungsmöglichkeiten und potential. In Setzen, F. (Hrsg) *Europapolitische kommunikation und Web 2.0 – formen, trends, herausforderungen und chancen*. Förderverein Europa Zentrum Baden-Württemberg.

O'Reilly, T. (2005). *What is web 2.0?: design patterns and business models for the next generation of software*. Retrieved from http://www.oreilly.de [16.06.2014].

Pavlik, J. V. (2007). *Mapping the consequences of technology on public relations*. Retrieved from http://www.instituteforpr.org [16.06.2014].

PEW Research. (2012). *Social networking popular across globe: arab publics most likely to express political views online*. Retrieved from http://www.pewglobal.org/files/2012/12/Pew-Global-Attitudes-Project-Technology-Report-FINAL-December-12-2012.pdf [16.06.2014].

Pleil, T. (2007). *Online-PR im web 2.0: fallbeispiele aus wirtschaft und politik*. Konstanz: UVK.

Rheingold, H. (1993). *The virtual community: homesteading on the electronic frontier*. Reading: Addison-Wesley.

Scheer, L. (1994). *La démocratie virtuelle*. Paris: Flammarion.

Schmidt, J. (2008). Was ist neu am social web?: soziologische und kommunikationswissenschaftliche grundlagen. In A. Zerfaß, M. Welker & J. Schmidt (Eds.), *Kommunikation, partizipation und wirkungen im social Web* (pp. 18-40). Köln: Halem.

Schweitzer, E. J. (2008). Innovation or normalization in e–campaigning? A longitudinal content and structural analysis of German party websites in the 2002 and 2005 national elections. *European Journal of Communication*, 23 (4): 449-470.

Schweitzer, E. J. (2011). Normalization 2.0: a longitudinal analysis of German online campaigns in the national elections 2002–9. *European Journal of Communication*, 26 (4): 310–327.

Seltzer, T. & Zhang, W. (2011). Toward a model of political organization-public relationships: antecedent and cultivation strategy influence on citizens' relationships with political parties. *Journal of Public Relations Research*, 23(1): 24-45.

Seltzer, T.; Zhang,W., Gearhart, S. & Conduff, L. (2013). Sources of citizens' experiential and reputational relationships with political parties. *Public Relations Journal*, 7(4).

Serra, J. P. (2012). Novos media e participação política. *Observatorio (OBS*) Journal*, 6 (2): 127-155.

Shane, P. (ed.) (2004). *Democracy online: the prospects for political renewal through the internet.* New York: Routledge.

Strömbäck, J. & Kiousis, S. (Eds.) (2011). *Political public relations: principles and applications.* New York: Routledge.

Sweetser, K. D. (2010). A losing strategy: the impact of nondisclosure in social media on relationships. *Journal of Public Relations Research*, 22(3): 288-312.

Sweetser, K. D. (2011). Digital political public relations. In J. Strömbäck & S. Kiousis (Eds.), *Political public relations: principles and applications* (pp. 293-313). New York: Routledge.

Sweetser, K. D. & Tedesco, J. C. (2014). Effects of exposure and messaging on political organization-public relationships exemplified in the candidate-constituent relationship. *American Behavioral Scientist*, 58(6): 776–793.

Taylor, M. & Kent, M. L. (2004). Congressional web sites and their potential for public dialogues. *Atlantic Journal of Communication*, 12(2): 59–76.

van Eimeren, B. & Frees, B. (2012). 76 Prozent der Deutschen online: neue nutzungssituationen durch mobile endgeräte: Ergebnisse der ARD&ZDF-Onlinestudie 2012. *Media Perspektiven*, 7(8): 362-379.

Wright, S. (2012). Politics as usual? Revolution, normalization and a new agenda for online deliberation, *New Media & Society*, 14(2): 244-261.

Zerfaß, A. (2007). Von der einkanal-kommunikation zum dialog wenn empfänger zu akteuren werden. In T. Ellerbeck & K. Siebenhaar (Eds.), *Vernetzte welt: veränderungen der kommunikation durch neue medien und mobilfunk* (pp. 31-48). Berlin: B & S Siebenhaar.

Chapter 7

The research project "New media and politics: citizens's participation in the websites of Portuguese political parties": main results

J. Paulo Serra and Gisela Gonçalves

Introduction

The "New media and politics: citizen participation in the websites of Portuguese political parties" project, funded by the Portuguese Foundation for Science and Technology[1], was carried out by a research group of the Online Communication Lab (LabCom) research centre at the University of Beira Interior (Portugal) between 1 March 2012 and 28 February 2015. The main objective of this chapter is to highlight the core components of the aforementioned project. A full description of the scientific framework of the project can be found in the published book *Political Participation and Web 2.0* (Serra *et al.*, 2014).

As the title implies, the concept of participation is a cornerstone of the project. Citizen participation has always been seen as a fundamental requisite for democracy, whatever model it takes: liberal, republican or deliberative (Habermas, 1994). At the same time, the "refeudalization" of the public sphere has also been understood as a major obstacle to citizens' political participation in our mediated societies (Habermas, 1989).

With the emergence and development of Web 2.0, we witnessed a renewed interest in the concept of participation as well as in the different forms it may take (Carpentier, 2011). This interest has substantially increased since the Obama election, in 2008, which has showed the internet website's potential to act as a hub in political-electoral campaigning, in regard to contact between parties / can-

[1] Reference PTDC/CCI-COM/122715/2010.

didates and citizens, the mobilization of members and supporters, the organization of rallies and other events, raising funds, etc. (Gomes *et al.*, 2009; Smith, 2009).

Nevertheless, studies from different countries have shown how the majority of political party and candidate websites tend to favour the informative function over the interactive and participative ones (Gibson, Margolis, Resnick & Ward, 2003; Schweitzer, 2005); they have also shown that, even when participation exists, this participation is predominantly seen as an instrument to project an image of credibility and/or arouse voters' sympathy, in a top-down logic (Rolfe, 2008). And what to think about the Portuguese case? When our research project was designed (2010), we did not know of any significant work in this area in Portugal.[2] At that time, and based on previous studies, we had the impression that, in general terms, three main obstacles existed to the development of a "digital democracy" in Portugal: the predominance of television in the media system; the political-parliamentary system – little contact with voters; citizens' lack of motivation for political participation (Cardoso, Cunha & Nascimento, 2003). Moreover, an exploratory study conducted on the Portuguese Parliament website about the use of Web 2.0 tools that aim to increase the interaction between Members of Parliament and citizens – forums, blogs, petitions – has seen little participation by either party (Serra, 2012).

It can be said that the Web 2.0 campaigns in Portugal began with the 2009 parliamentary elections. In these elections, the two largest Portuguese parties, the Socialist Party (PS) and the Social-Democrat Party (PSD) (government and opposition, respectively, at that time), launched the "Movimento Sócrates 2009" website (on 2 March 2009) and the "Política de Verdade" website (28 April 2009). The former, the PS website, was clearly inspired by the Obama campaign. They even hired the company Blue State Digital (BSD), which was responsible for organizing and managing the Obama online campaign (see Rodrigues, 2015).

A campaign is a campaign, however. It is a period when parties and candidates mobilize all the material and human resources they have. But what about the periods between campaigns, the so-called "normal" periods? Do political parties use their websites to enable and foster citizens' participation? And do citizens participate? And

[2] Later, there was a master's dissertation (Silva, 2012), which focused on the interactivity of Portuguese political parties' websites during non-electoral periods, performing a content analysis of those websites.

what kind of participation are we speaking of? In fact, the concept of participation is complex and elusive; it can be used with different meanings in different contexts (Dahlgren, 2011).

In the specific context of this project, by "participation" we mean the actions performed by citizens using internet tools, especially Web 2.0 tools (blogs, Facebook, etc.), and through which they can create and share political content and get involved in social networks (Smith & Rainie, 2008). Narrowing our concept even further, we were interested in the participation that citizens have through/on the websites of Portuguese political parties during non-electoral periods.

However, real participation is different from access and interaction because of "the key role that is attributed to power, and to equal(ized) power relations in decision-making processes." (Carpentier, 2011, p. 29). Hence, we were also interested in finding out if those forms of participation constituted real political participation, with some impact and consequences on the political parties' agendas (themes, actions) or if, on the contrary, they were only a mere simulation of participation with mere propagandistic intentions. That is to say that citizens' participation is not enough; the response that political parties give to that participation is a key factor.

Method

Based on the theoretical framework, the research problem guiding the project was as follows: 'What is the degree of correspondence between the participation that the websites of the Portuguese political parties allow citizens and citizens' expectations about their participation – in non-electoral periods?' In this context, the expression "Portuguese political parties" only includes the parties which had (and have) parliamentary representation: CDS/PP – Democratic Social Centre/Popular Party (Christian democrats, office-seeking, ideological party);[3] PSD – Social Democratic Party (vote-seeking, catch-all party); PS – Socialist Party (vote-seeking, catch-all

[3] To globally characterize these political parties, we use Strom's distinction between policy-seeking, vote-seeking and office-seeking parties (Strom, 1990) and Kirchheimer's distinction between ideological and catch-all parties (Kirchheimer, 1966). As we know, all these classifications are relative and not fully applicable to all situations. About these classifications of the Portuguese political parties, see also Belchior & Freire, 2012.

party); PCP – Portuguese Communist Party (Marxist, policy-seeking, ideological party); BE – Left Bloc (Marxist, policy-seeking, ideological party). It also must be added that, throughout our research project, the Portuguese government was ruled by a coalition composed of the CDS-PP and the PSD, which had the majority of seats at the Parliament, with the PS, PCP and BE parties in opposition.

From that general problem, three main research questions (RQ) emerged:

RQ1. What are the participatory tools available to citizens on Portuguese political parties' websites? How do Portuguese political parties interact with citizens via the participatory internet tools available on their websites?

RQ2. What is the opinion of the leaders of Portuguese political parties and the communication managers about the citizens' participation on their websites? Does this participation involve any change to the political party agenda (themes, actions)?

RQ3. What are citizens' opinions about the possibility of entering into interaction with parties via their websites? How do they evaluate their own participation on the websites?

In relation to our research problem, and based upon our literature review, we admitted the general hypothesis that there was a lack of correspondence between the participation that the websites of the Portuguese political parties allow citizens and citizens' expectations about it. As more specific research questions, we defined the following hypotheses:

H1. Citizen participation tends to favour image-based forms of expression (videos, photos), is predominantly supportive (not critical) of the political party, and tends not to depend on the political-ideological orientation of the party.

H2. The leaders of the parties and the people responsible for the management of their websites tend to see citizen participation more as an instrument of delivering their own message than as a way of listening to citizens' messages.

H3. The citizens expect the websites of the political parties to be more open (with fewer constraints) to their participation, and to have more of an impact on the agenda and plans of the political parties.

To answer our research questions, and "falsify" (Popper) our hypotheses, we chose a methodological design based upon what Denzin (1970) calls triangulation, in a triple sense: methodological triangulation, i.e. the use of different methods for gathering data; data triangulation, i.e. the use of different sources of data; and, in certain cases, investigator triangulation, i.e. the investigation and interpretation of the same topic by different researchers. More specifically, initially, the following research techniques were planned:

1. *Content analysis* – to examine what tools are provided by the Portuguese political parties' websites for citizens to create and share political content and get involved in social networks (research question 1). This content analysis examined the websites of the five Portuguese parties that have parliamentary representation (CDS-PP, PSD, PS, PCP-Verdes, BE).

1.1. Complementarily, and based on the understanding of the importance that social networks in general and Facebook in particular have for the websites of the political parties, we did a content analysis of the three parties profile on Facebook – BE, PS and PSD (the PCP does not have an official Facebook profile and the Facebook page for the CDS/PP is in fact, for its leader, and was completely out of date).

1.2. In addition to the content analysis, and in order to understand how citizens can use the online participatory tools available on political websites, an "interaction experiment" was implemented. By creating 3 virtual identities (positive, negative and neutral), the interaction with political parties via websites was tested to check if the tools for participation available were truly effective, and to what extent. For example: if we send an e-mail, do we receive an answer? And how long do we have to wait for that answer?

2. *Semi-structured interviews* with the five political party leaders and the five communication managers to find out their opinions about citizens' participation on their websites (research question 2). With the interviews, it was expected to determine whether or not the agendas of the political parties (in terms of themes and actions) include citizens' participation on the websites and, if so, how this is implemented.

3. *Internet-based survey* – to find out citizens' opinions about their participation on the websites of the Portuguese political parties, an internet-based survey, using open source tools like Lime Survey[4], was addressed to a sample of five hundred Portuguese users of the political parties' websites (research question 3).

---

[4] Lime SurveLime Website (`http://www.limesurvey.org/`)

3.1. To complement the survey – since we had fewer responses than we expected – a focus group was organized with a convenience sample of undergraduate and graduate (Master's and PhD) students from the University of Beira Interior.

The application of all the research techniques is further detailed in the next section, in which we present and reflect on the main results of the project.

Main results

As several methods were implemented, this section presents each research technique in detail and discusses the main results obtained.

Content analysis

The objective of the content analysis was to examine the tools that the websites of the Portuguese political parties provide the citizens for them create and share political content and get involved in social networks.

The content analysis of the political parties' websites was performed over a period of one month (May 2013) and involved the five Portuguese parties that have parliamentary representation: CDS/PP – Democratic Social Centre/Popular Party; PSD – Social Democratic Party; PS – Socialist Party; PCP – Portuguese Communist Party; BE – Left Bloc.

Based on a preliminary study, a recording and analysis model was created to identify and characterize the websites' participatory tools (see López del Ramo, 2014, particularly pp. 265-272). The data was collected between 1 March 2012 and 5 October 2012 (López del Ramo, p. 245), and was presented and discussed at the international conference "Political Participation and Web 2.0", at the University of Beira Interior, on 11 and 12 October 2012.[5]

Using the recording model, all tools that give the public an active role were considered and analysed in relation to three dimensions: presence, visibility and functionality. In Table 7.1, we can see

[5] Further information about the first conference of the research project can be found here: `http://www.political-participation-web.ubi.pt/`

the example of the PS website, which had "the greatest number of participatory resources of the five websites studied", with access to blogs the only aspect missing (López del Ramo, 2014, p. 256):

Resource	Presence-Variety[6 7]	Visibility	Functionality
Contact details	100%	100% (3/3)	50% (3/6)
Comments	65%	33% (1/3)	71.4% (5/6)
Suggestions/enquiries	82.5%	33% (1/3)	57.1% (4/7)
Social networks	100%	100% (3/3)	100% (3/3)
Blogs	No	No	No
Surveys	82.5%	66.6% (2/3)	60% (3/5)
Chat/debates	82.5%	100%	57.1% (4/7)
RSS Syndication	82.5%	100% (3/3)	-
Average	74.3%[8]	76% (3)	65.9% [9]

Table 7.1: Adequacy level of PS participatory resources. Source: López del Ramo, 2014, p. 256

Resource	Usage ratio	Visibility[10]	Functionality	Overall treatment [11]
Contact details	100% PSD, CDS-PP, PCP, BE, PS	53.1%	73.3%	75.4%
Comments	80% PSD, CDS-PP, BE, PS	49.6%	70.2%	66.6%
Suggestions/ enquiries	100% PSD, CDS-PP, PCP, BE, PS	53.1%	71.4%	74.8%
Social networks	100% PSD, CDS-PP, PCP, BE, PS	93.3%	86.6%	93.3%
Blogs	0%	No	No	-
Surveys	20% PS	66.6%	60%	48.8%
Chat/debates	20% PS	100%	57.1%	59%
RSS Syndication	80% CDS-PP, PCP, BE, PS	79.1%	-	79.5%

Table 7.2: Adequacy levels of participatory resource on the range of websites studied. Source: López del Ramo, 2014, p. 257

The analysis of the participatory resources present on the websites of the five parties shows the overall results as presented in Table 7.3:

[6] According to the PV calculation formula PV= (E x 65/100) + (S x 35/100)

[7] E factor – Inclusion of the resource on the website; S factor – diversity of subtypes or variants (López del Ramo, p.251).

[8] Calculation obtained in relation to the total number of possible resources, whether they are found on the website or not

[9] Calculation obtained in relation to the resources found on the website

[10] Calculation obtained from the sum of all the websites on which this participatory resource is found.

[11] The average is obtained from the Usage ratio, Visibility and Functionality.

Party	Aspects			Total
	Presence-Variety[12]	Visibility	Functionality	
PSD	43.4%	41.1%	77.9%	54.1%
CDS-PP	52.2%	56.5%	85.1%	64.6%
PCP	42.6%	66.6%	78.5%	62.5%
BE	52.2%	73.2%	67.8%	64.4%
PS	74.3%	76%	65.9%	71.9%
Average	52.9%	62.6%	75%	63.5%

Table 7.3: Adequacy level for participatory resources by category. Source: López del Ramo, 2014, p. 259

Summing up, the overall results of the content analysis were as follows (see López del Ramo, 2014, pp. 260-2):

- Despite differences in number and characteristics, all websites included participatory tools (presence dimension).
- Only 3 of the 8 tools were implemented on all websites: contact details, suggestions and social media.
- Comments and RSS syndication existed on 4 websites (Comments: PSD, CDS-PP, BE, PS; RSS: CDS-PP, PCP, BE, PS).
- Forum/chat was present on only one website (PS).
- None of the websites included a blog.
- Social media was the most common interactive tool and the most visible (visibility dimension).
- The websites are ranked higher in regard to functionality, because they are generally clear and simple to use, although their visibility could be significantly improved.

In terms of political parties, the PS website clearly stands out from the others in regard to all aspects; nonetheless, the adequacy score for all websites exceeds the 50% threshold.

The website with the lowest overall score is the PSD website, but also there are significant negative points on both the BE and PCP websites. The former for its inconsistent structure, since it actually comprises one main website and three independent sub-websites,

[12]According to the PV calculation formula PV= (E x 65/100) + (S x 35/100)

which creates dispersion and a certain incoherence in the participatory resources. For the PCP website, the lack of comments or its own profile on social media gives it a restrictive and opaque nature that does not fit the naturally open approach of Web 2.0. (López del Ramo, 2014, pp. 261-2).

The data collected in an exploratory study about the comments section showed a trend towards a lack of participation (publication) and a very low frequency of comments as well. One explanation for the low number and frequency of comments, and the almost non-existence of debates, may be the transfer of political opinion debate to the social media environment, particularly Facebook. This hypothesis was further analysed in a content analysis of Facebook and the interaction experiment that is described below.

Facebook content analysis

One of the results of the content analysis of the websites of the five political parties was that social networks were "the best-treated participatory resource, whose score is close to what may be considered optimal level [..], which is in itself an enlightening result in terms of the value assigned to them by parties as a political tool" (López del Ramo, 2014, p. 261). Among those social networks, Facebook was clearly the most important.[13] This result therefore fully justified a content analysis of the way the different political parties used Facebook.

The Facebook content analysis focused only on the BE, PSD and PS. It did not consider the CDS-PP for two reasons. Firstly, because despite being included on the party website, the Facebook page was not for the CDS/PP, but rather for the party leader, Paulo Portas, and secondly, because it was not updated (the last post was made on 7 July 2011). The content analysis also did not consider the PCP because the party did not have an official Facebook page.

The analysis took place from 6 May to 21 June 21 2013 and analysed a total of 26 days, distributed over the following weeks: 31 December to 6 January; 4 to 10 February; 11 to 17 March; 22 to 26 April (27 and 28 April were excluded, due to the PS convention).

[13] According to a recent report, in 2013, 98.0% of the Portuguese users of social networks had a profile on Facebook, 13.7% on Google+, 10.4% on Hi5, 9.0% on Twitter, 7.5% on LinkedIn, and 3.2% on Badoo (Cardoso *et al.*, 2014, p. 16).

The analysis categories for each post were: Date, Author, Title / Theme, Semiosis (text, photo, video, etc., alone or as an addition), Likes, Comments, Shares, Authors of the comments (Sex: M – men, W – women, NI – not identified), Tone of the comments (F – favourable to the party, U – unfavourable to the party, N – neutral to the party), and S – Comments with suggestions for the party (initiatives, actions, strategies).

The questions raised in the analysis were:

i) What are the characteristics of the messages posted by political parties, in terms of their political authors, topics, and semiotic characteristics?

(ii) Does the frequency of citizens' participation depend on their gender (as apparent in the comments)?

(iii) Does the frequency of citizens' participation depend on the political-ideological orientation (right/left) of the parties?

(iv) Is citizens' participation determined by their previous, existing political attitudes (those who are "already convinced")?

(v) Do citizens' comments include suggestions for political initiatives?

First of all, we present the overall results of the Facebook analysis in regard to Posts, Likes, Comments and Shares. For each party, we show the total for the 26 days and the average per day:

		Posts	**Likes**	**Comments**	**Shares**
BE	Total	104	3158	202	3149
	Average	4	121.46	7.76	121.11
PS	Total	84	12233	1680	3200
	Average	3.23	470.5	64.61	123.07
PSD	Total	76	2620	318	1095
	Average	2.92	100.76	12.23	42.11

Table 7.4: Posts: Party

As we can see, all parties published an average of between 2.9 and 4 posts per day.

The BE was the most active party in terms of posts, both in total number and daily average, followed by the PS and the PSD; however, in terms of Likes, Comments and Shares, the PS was in first place, followed by the BE in Likes and Shares, and the PSD in Comments.

i) Characteristics of the political parties' posts

Our first research question was: What are the characteristics of the messages posted by political parties, in terms of their political authors, topics, and semiotic characteristics? The data follows below.

Authors and topics

The authors of the posts were exclusively members of the party organization, their leaders and their colleagues. The main author was, undoubtedly, the party leader. Citizens could not post, only comment. Consequently, the topics of the posts were invariably linked to the life of the party and its positions on the several political questions at stake.

Semiosis

As we can see in Table 7.5, most posts consisted of text + photograph (53.79%), followed by text only (15.91%), text+video (12.5%), text+poster (9.09%), and text+icon (5.68%), while the other forms barely registered. If we consider all the posts that are not exclusively composed of text, i.e. those that include any kind of image, we have a result of 84.09%. As regards parties, the PS does not use text only, and the PSD is the party that has the greatest proportion of text-only posts (almost a third of all its posts).

ii) Characteristics of citizens' comments

The other research questions we posed dealt with the characteristics of citizens' participation (comments) on the political parties' Facebook pages in regard to: a) the relationship between the frequency of citizens' participation and their gender (as apparent in the comments), their political-ideological leaning (right/left), and their previous, existing political attitudes (the "already convinced"); b) the inclusion of suggestions for political initiatives.

	BE	PS	PSD	Total	Per cent
photo+graph	1	0	0	1	0.38
text	18	0	24	42	15.91
text+diagram	1	0	0	1	0.38
text+front page+photo	0	0	2	2	0.76
text+icon	0	2	13	15	5.68
text+photo	59	58	25	142	53.79
text+poster	12	8	4	24	9.09
text+poster+photo	2	0	0	2	0.76
text+postit	0	0	2	2	0.76
text+video	11	16	6	33	12.50
Total	104	84	76	264	100.00

Table 7.5: Posts: Semiosis

Ideology/gender

Table 7.6 shows that, in ideological terms, the PS has an overwhelming number of comments compared to the BE and the PSD, and that men comment much more than women (74.97% versus 22.61%). Cross-referencing both categories, ideology and gender, we see that the participation decreases from left to right (BE – 34.52%, PS – 21.46%, and PSD – 18.30%).

		Men[14]	Women	Not identified	Total
BE	Total	122	68	7	197
	Per cent	61.93%	34.52%	3.55%	100%
PS	Total	1119	315	34	1468
	Per cent	76.23%	21.46%	2.31%	100%
PSD	Total	122	28	3	153
	Per cent	79.74%	18.30%	1.96%	100%
	Total	1363	411	44	1818
	Per cent	74.97%	22.61%	2.42%	100.00%

Table 7.6: Comments: Ideology/Gender

[14] Gender was determined by the name of the author of the comments

Party/tone

Overall, as shown in Table 7.7, the comments are more favourable than unfavourable or neutral, and suggestions form the category with the lowest value (only 0.31%). This may lead us to conclude that the participants are mainly the "already convinced", i.e. members and supporters of the political parties. However, when we look at each of the three parties, we see that while in regard to the BE the comments were overwhelmingly favourable (81.73%), in regard to the PS they were only slightly favourable (38.22%), and in regard to the PSD they were more unfavourable (40.53%). We can explain the results of the PS by the fact – empirically evinced in the comments – that its leader at the time (António José Seguro) was not fully accepted by the party. The results of the PSD can be explained by the fact that the coalition of which it was part, which took power on 21 June 2011, had taken severe measures to fight the economic and financial crisis that began in 2008, which the members of the party themselves disliked.

		Favourable	**Unfavourable**	**Neutral**	**Suggestions**[15]	**Total**
BE	Total	161	12	24	0	197
	Per cent	81.73%	6.09%	12.18%	0	100%
PS	Total	561	460	414	33	1468
	Per cent	38.22%	31.34%	28.20%	2.24%	100%
PSD	Total	42	62	40	9	153
	Per cent	27.45%	40.53%	26.14%	5.88%	100
	Total	764	534	478	42	1818
	Per cent	42.03%	29.37%	26.29%	2.31%	100.00

Table 7.7: Comments: Party/Tone

Moreover, with these quantitative results, we must note that dialogue, when it took place in the comments, was not between party and commenters, but rather among the commenters themselves – usually among those who defended and those who attacked the party's position. And this was more frequent on the PSD Facebook page than on the BE page; the number of those attacking the party was higher on the former as well.

[15] Independently of whether they were favourable, unfavourable or neutral.

Interaction experiment

To understand how citizens can use online participatory tools available on political parties' websites (for example: if we send an e-mail, do we receive a reply? How long do we have to wait to receive that reply?), we carried out an interaction experiment. To implement this experiment, three different (fictitious) virtual identities were created, each with a different position regarding the party: negative, neutral, and positive.

The experiment took place over a month, from 1 to 31 May 2013, and was implemented by a group of post-graduate students and one project researcher.[16] The interaction was tested by e-mail, comments and suggestions, both on the website and on the Facebook page. Later, the interaction with each party was described and analysed in a succinct report. It is these five reports that constitute the basis of the conclusions we summarize next. Before discussing those conclusions, we present the example of the profiles created to interact with the CDS-PP:[17]

1. Neutral profile (Alberto Ferreira)

Email:
Good afternoon,
I was reading about the budget cuts that the government plans for 2014.
I wonder what the CDS' opinion on the subject is.
Sincerely,

Alberto Ferreira
ferreira.alberto@outlook.com
Sent 5 May, 9:35am

Suggestion:
Good morning,

[16] Master's students: Felipe Bonow Soares, Gonçalo Morais, Joana Morais, Lurdes Rocha; PhD student: Rosália Rodrigues.

[17] These profiles, like the others, were created by our Master's student Felipe Bonow Soares, and were used after being analysed and discussed by the research group.

I have doubts about the government's economic plans.[18] I would like to suggest that the CDS publish a document with details and the party's opinion.
Alberto Ferreira

Sent 23 May, 11:05am

Comment:
I couldn't tell if that is the MEP's way of thinking or also the party's... What is the CDS' position?

Sent 13 May, 2:40pm

[18] As has been stated before, at the time, the Portuguese government was formed of a CDS-PP-PSD coalition.

2. Positive profile (José Machado):

Email:

Dear friends of the CDS,

The latest news I read about the position of the CDS-PP on the need to think about the economy and not just about finance made me feel good. I agree with the party's position. We need a change of attitude!

Best regards,

José Machado

machadojose833@gmail.com

Sent 3 May, 9pm

Suggestion:

Friends,

I was reading about Paulo Portas'[19] position on pensioners. I share the party's view. I suggest you continue to defend the interests of pensioners in Portugal.

Best regards,

José Machado

Sent (with error) 8 May, 3:15pm, 10 May, 10:35pm, 13 May, 1:35pm and 16 May, 1:30pm

Sent (without error) 22 May, 9:55pm

Comment:

Friends, I agree with Nuno's[20] speech. The CDS is trying to rebuild Portugal in the best possible way. Join the CDS for a better Portugal. Congratulations!

Sent 27 May,10:25am

3. Negative profile (Maria Francisca Arruda):

Email:

Good morning,

---

[19] Paulo Portas was, at the time, the leader of the CDS-PP.

[20] Nuno Melo, a CDS-PP Member of the European Parliament and a very influential member of the party.

I see more and more contradictions in the government and disagreements between the PSD and the CDS/PP. I honestly don't know how internal problems can help our country to end the crisis. I hope for a change in government for the good of the Portuguese people.
Maria Francisca Arruda

mfarruda01@hotmail.com
Sent 3 May, 6:45pm

Suggestion:
This no longer working! The PSD-CDS government is not getting along. I suggest you rethink your attitudes and unite again for the sake of Portugal! Or separate immediately! But make a decision and have a proper discourse.

Sent 23 May, 3:30pm

Comment:
I disagree with Abel Baptista's[21] position. The CDS has to change its position. We need to think more about the people and get closer to the people!

Sent 25 May, 9:50pm

About the main conclusions of our interaction experiment, we can say that overall the 5 websites had very low levels of interaction; in one case, there was no interaction (CDS/PP) and in another contact was only available via e-mail produced feedback (PCP). All the websites enabled contact via e-mail after registration, however, only two parties actually replied to the e-mail (PSD and PCP). In the case of the PSD, the reply came from a PR professional. In the case of the PS website, the e-mail address did not work.

Of the 3 websites that allowed comments (for example, on news or videos), only one (PS) published them. However, comments did not receive any answer and the negative comment was deleted/censored after a short period. In the comments section, the only interaction was between website users (horizontal communication) and there was no official reply from the political party.

[21] An important member of the CDS-PP who was a Member of the Portuguese Parliament.

Interviews

At the beginning of the project, ten interviews were planned with the five leaders of the political parties and their communication managers. However, due to scheduling problems – and also interest, in fact – only the interviews with the communication managers went ahead. In certain cases, it was also very difficult to arrange a meeting.

The semi-structured interviews with the communication managers of the five political parties, which took place in Lisbon between 4 February and 3 April 2014, lasted between 30 minutes and one hour and were digitally recorded and transcribed for accuracy. The interviews aimed to find out their opinion about the use of participatory tools on websites, and confront them with the data collected through the content analysis and interaction experiment (see the interview questions in Appendix 1).

First of all, Table 7.8 summarizes the main characteristics of the communication management structure of the five political parties:

	BE	PCP	PS	PSD	CDS
Communication management	Team: 7	Team: 4	Team: 4	Team: 7	Team: 3
Most important social media	Facebook Twitter	YouTube (not on Facebook)	Facebook	Facebook, Twitter, Flickr, YouTube, Instagram	Facebook (closed group, not official)
Comment moderation	Comments with offensive language forbidden/deleted				
Emphasized functions	Information	Information – disintermediation [22]	Information – disintermediation	Information – contact with the militants	Interaction
Integration of citizens' suggestions	No	No	No	No	Yes

Table 7.8: Communication management structure

Communication management team: with the exception of the PS, which at the time of the interview had a professional communication director who was not affiliated with the party, the parties' management teams were directed and composed of members and/or supporters of the party, some as volunteers.

Social media: for all the parties, with the remarkable exception of the PCP (which prefers YouTube), the most important social network was Facebook, which tends to be where the discussion that could have taken place on the website is held. However, all the parties consider that it is virtually impossible to develop a systematic process of interaction and discussion with citizens on Face-

[22] In the sense of sending the message directly to citizens, bypassing the traditional media and journalists.

book, due to a lack of time and/or human resources. This confirms our own content analysis which showed that citizens interact with citizens on the social network commenting on other commenters' comments, rather than interacting with the parties.

Comment moderation: all the parties say that they do not have the time or human resources necessary to perform this task; the only moderation that exists involves erasing or not publishing comments that use offensive language. However, as we saw in the section on the interaction experiment, there was a comment by one of the members of our project that was erased by one of the parties not because it was offensive but because it was unfavourable (critical) to the party.

Emphasized functions: as discussed below, all the parties tended to emphasize the function of their website to provide information on their history, initiatives, proposals, etc. not only for members, supporters, and citizens in general but also for journalists. Functions that are Web 2.0 specific, like interaction, discussion, participation, etc. only come in second place. In a certain sense, it is as if the parties had Web 2.0 tools – social networks, blogs, etc. – only to attract citizens, and do not make them function in an effective way.

Integration of citizens' suggestions: in line with what has been said, and with the exception of the CDS/PP, all the parties confess that they do not integrate citizens' suggestions into their plans or proposals – mostly because they have not enough time and resources to read and consider those suggestions.

The analysis of the interview transcripts employed a broad thematic discourse framework, in which findings were based on the recurrent themes, patterns and categories that surfaced in the discourse (Deacon *et al.*, 2007). Conclusions were drawn by comparing the thematic findings from all interviews. The representative quotations provided are in italic type and have been edited into a narrative form (i.e. repetitions and interjections removed) for ease of understanding.

Three main themes emerged regarding how the five political communication managers perceive and recommend the use of the participatory tools available on political websites: 1. Information and disintermediation; 2. Private answers to public questions; 3. Fostering web users' discussions.

Information and disintermediation

All interviewees acknowledge the central role played by the online media in the political parties' current communication strategies. They view websites as structural elements in the parties' information strategies, as an essential means to disseminate political standpoints quickly and, above all, without third-party mediation. That is, avoiding possible distortion of the message – something that is usually called "disintermediation". As some of the communication managers stressed:

> *Online vehicles let us tell the story exactly as it is. Most people in their daily lives read about the political situation in the media, which in turn have filters. On our channels, we present the situation exactly as it is for us, the message as we believe it should be conveyed to our audience, whether they are members or not.* (PS)
>
> *Right now, the strategy is to be more informative rather than to engage people in discussion. For people to realize what we are doing. The discussion is on the TSF forums, SIC, TVI 24 etc., and not on our FB.* [...] *We now have another concern, which is to reach out to younger people (16-18 and 25): they are very alienated from politics. There is a deficit of information and political training. In the future, we want to develop a Facebook strategy for youth, through civic messages to test those involved.* (PSD)

Disintermediation does not mean interaction, however. In fact, the communication managers acknowledge that their parties do not have the conditions – time, space and human resources – necessary to establish real interaction with citizens. The quantity and diversity of citizens' questions make interaction and discussion with them an almost impossible task. As two of the communication managers emphasize:

> *I wish we had time to interact but, right now, we have neither the time nor the space on Facebook to do so.* (PS)
>
> *The greatest difficulty in managing interaction lies in the amount of requests, comments, but also in the vastness of issues that citizens raise with us. Everyone has a different concern. It is very difficult to answer to all of*

> *them, there are too many topics. With the resources we have here it is very complicated. We don't have an army behind the machine!* (PSD)

Private answers to public questions

As we saw in the previous section, parties do not reply to (comment on) the comments posted by citizens. However, they say that this does not mean they do not answer those comments – only they do so in private. In doing so, they aim to avoid online discussions that can be confusing, controversial and quickly get out of control. So, what we have here is a kind of inversion: (public) parties answer public questions from (private) citizens with private answers. In the words of some communication managers:

> *We do not react because we do not want people to feel that we are limiting their discussion.* (BE)
>
> *We choose not to debate issues on Facebook (...) It is too much of a risk to start a dialogue with citizens and have to justify standpoints. It would be a never-ending discussion.* (PSD)

Therefore, the main objective of each party website and its different tools is, in the words of the communication managers, to observe and monitor the on-going discussions among the citizens, how they react to the party's proposals, what they think about different political issues, etc., i.e. to function as what Luhmann terms an "observing system". An observing system that, in the future, should provide the party with the kind of reflexivity that observing systems are made for.

Fostering web users' discussions

The communication managers of all parties acknowledge that the websites and their tools, besides providing information and allowing interaction, foster online discussion. However, they do not necessarily equate this online discussion with political participation. It could even be the case that online discussion is seen as contradictory with (real) political participation, as in the case of the PCP:

> *Effective political participation cannot be mostly through digital channels. However, these channels may add something and provide an incentive, because of the information they make available (...) An interesting aspect for those who study these areas lies in the reverse situation: I believe that it would not be impossible to empirically prove that in many circumstances these [online] instruments are a factor in reduced participation.* (PCP)

In fact, if we remember the concept of participation discussed in the introduction, participation involves power, that is to say, the possibility of contributing to changing things. One way of doing that would be for parties to integrate citizens' contributions into their plans, proposals and initiatives. However, this is a major problem for all parties, with the remarkable exception of the CDS/PP:

> *The main problem is that we do not have time to choose relevant things.* (BE)
>
> [...] *When we made these forums, we often took ideas for ... even for our proposals, here at the Assembly, draft resolutions, and working groups within the party. We took several ideas. I wouldn't say that we took all of them, that would not be true, but we took several ideas, even for the birth group, several things, for the fiscal area...* (CDS-PP)

Internet-based survey

The objective of the internet-based survey was to find out citizens' opinion about their own use of the participatory tools on political parties' websites. The questionnaire was created on the Lime Survey platform[23] hosted at Labcom (www.labcom.ubi.pt), and was available during two different periods: between 1 February and 11 May 2014 and between 4 December and 8 January 2015.

The survey population was composed of Portuguese citizens aged over 18, living in Portugal or abroad. The selection of the sample of respondents was made using a "snowball technique", asking a first group of five people to send the invitation to another five people as diverse as possible in terms of education, income, residence,

[23] `https://www.inqueritos.ubi.pt/admin/admin.php`

etc., and so on. The questionnaire was completed in such a way that the respondents could remain anonymous. We obtained 135 complete questionnaires in the first period, and 94 complete questionnaires in the second one, totalizing 229 complete questionnaires; we should also mention that in both periods there were 14 incomplete questionnaires, which were discarded, thus making a total of 243 questionnaires received.

The questionnaire included two different parts: I. A. Characteristics of the respondent -aimed to identify the socio-demographic characteristics of the respondents; B. participation in the political parties' websites – directed only towards those who had answered in part A that they visit political parties' websites; aimed to record their participation on the websites (for the full questionnaire, see Appendix 2).

Below, we present the socio-demographic characteristics of the respondents, and the main results found about citizens' participation in political parties' websites.

Socio-demographic characteristics of the respondents

As we can see in Appendix 3, our sample of respondents included a very similar percentage of men and women (48.47% and 51.53% respectively). They were mostly aged 18 to 35 and 36 to 50 (33.19% and 52.40% respectively), held a higher education degree (Bachelor's degree – 27.51%, Master's degree – 27.07%, and PhD – 37.12%), were predominantly single or married (33.19% and 44.98% respectively), lived in a household with 1 to 4 members, in the north or centre of Portugal (31.88% and 38.86% respectively; however, 24.45% live in the south, Lisbon, Alentejo or the Algarve), worked in the public sector (57.21%), as specialists in intellectual and scientific professions (55.02%), and had an individual income of less than 2,000 euros (monthly net income).

As regards information technologies, all the respondents said they had a computer at home, in most cases a laptop. Almost all said they had a broadband internet connection at home (94.76%) and used internet every day (92.58%), mostly at home or at their place of work/study. This data from the sample is consistent with the data provided by the last official reports concerning Portuguese citizens in general, which showed that at the end of 2014, 63% of households in Portugal had a broadband internet connection (only

2% had no broadband internet), and that 65% of people aged between 16 and 74 accessed the internet. These values were 98% and 98% respectively for those aged 16 to 24 years, and 97% and 97% for those with higher education (while internet use is inversely proportional to age and directly proportional to users' academic qualifications). Among students, the amounts reached 100% and 99% respectively. As for the equipment used to access the internet, a laptop computer was used in 88% of households (INE, 2014). The data also showed that most Portuguese internet users used it on a daily basis (Cardoso *et al.*, 2014).

Regarding political engagement, most of the respondents said they were not members of a political party (89.52%); however, the sample was divided almost in half between those who support and those who do not support a party (51.09% supporters, 48.91% non-supporters). Of the respondents that said they were members or supporters, the highest percentage belonged to the PS (6.11% members, 23.14% supporters).

As it turns out, the people included in the sample were almost entirely heavy internet users and, taking into account their age, education and occupation, they had the greatest tendency to participate on political parties' websites.

Citizens' participation on political parties' websites

Only 20.09% (N=46) of the people in the sample of internet users said they visited political parties' websites, while 79.91% (N=183) said they did not. (Percentage of N=229)

As we can see in Table 7.9, of the 46 visitors, an average of 4.35% said they visited the websites every day, 7.39% several days a week, 14.79% one day a week, 48.70% rarely, and 24.78% never visited them. (However, seemingly contradictorily, there is an average of 24.78% respondents who said they never visited parties' websites; in the question visit/not visit, however, they had said that they visited them).

Frequency/Parties' websites[24]	BE	PCP	PS	PSD	Average	CDS
1. Never	26.09	23.91	4.35	34.78	34.78	24.78%
2. Rarely	56.52	56.52	50	36.96	43.48	48.70%
3. One day a week	8.7	8.7	21.74	19.57	15.22	14.79%
4. Several days a week	6.52	8.7	15.22	4.35	2.17	7.39%
5. Every day	2.17	2.17	8.7	4.35	4.35	4.35%
No answer	0	0	0	0	0	0%
TOTAL	100	100	100.01	100.01	100	100.00%

Table 7.9: Frequency of visits to parties' websites (%)

When we consider the sum of the categories "3. One day a week", "4. Several days a week", and "5. Every day", we have an average of 26.53% for all parties. Looking to each party in turn, the PS has the best results (45.66%), followed by the PSD (28.27%), the CDS/PP (21.74%), the PCP (19.57%) and the BE (17.39%).

What are the reasons for visiting the websites? A content analysis of the open answers shows that they mostly visited to update political information (73.91%), with low percentages mentioning civic participation/support for the party (8.7%), or research (8.7%); 8.7% indicated other/different reasons. (Percentage of N=46 respondents).

What are the reasons for not visiting? Most did not visit because they had no interest in politics (52.46%), preferring to receive political information via the mass media, mainly TV (19.1%), distrusting in politics (10.38%), considering websites propagandistic and biased (4.92%), or not having enough time to visit them (2.73%); there was also a percentage of respondents that indicated other/different reasons (10.38%, with each category equal to or less than 4). (Percentage of N=183 respondents).

What do respondents do when they visit the political parties' websites? They mainly e-mailed the party (17.17% citations), participated in social networks (Facebook, etc.) (15.15%), and made comments (14.14%). Other less cited actions were making suggestions (6.06%), sending pictures (4.04%), volunteering for party actions such as meetings, rallies, etc. (4.04%), participating in forums (4.04%), joining the party (4.04%), participating in chats (2.02%), sending videos (1.01%), and making donations (1.01%). There was a percentage of respondents who did other, unspecified actions (27.27%) which we think are mainly to do with information-seeking activities. (Percentage of N=99, multiple answers of the 46 respondents).

[24] We do not consider "other" here (other than the parties that our research focused on).

When asked how often political agents react to their contact (by e-mail, comments), respondents answered never (45.65%), sometimes (36.96%), often (4.35%), and always (13.04%). (Percentage of N=46 respondents).

Regarding the way political parties answer citizens, the respondents said that they used e-mail (51.35%), replies to their comments on posts (16.22%), replies to their suggestions (5.41%), replies to their comment on a news story (2.70%), and other, unspecified ways (24.32%). (Percentage of N=37, multiple answers of the 25 respondents that did not answer "never" in the previous question).

Which political parties' Facebook pages had respondents already visited? The top site was the PS website (28.97%), followed by the websites of the PSD and the BE (each of them with 17.93%), the PCP (13.10%), the CDS/PP (11.72%), and Others (10.34%). More important than the percentage each party got is the fact that they all were or had been visited by citizens. (Percentage of N=145, multiple answers of the 46 respondents).

Do you usually share or comment on news you read on the parties? websites on social networks (e.g. Facebook)? To this question, 34.78% of the respondents answered yes, and 65.22% answered no. (Percentage of N=46).

What about the usefulness of the parties' websites as a means of communicating with citizens? Respondents believed that they were not very useful (10.87%), somewhat useful (19.57%), useful (45.65%), or very useful (23.91%). (Percentage of N=46 respondents).

What are the websites useful for? According to the content of our respondents' answers, most mentioned obtaining information or getting more in-depth information about the political parties (56.4%), encouraging closer contact and direct communication with the parties (23.1%), allowing citizens to participate politically/exercise citizenship (5.13%), or other, varied reasons (15.38%). (Percentage of N=39).

Focus Group

To complement the information obtained in the online survey,[25] and bearing in mind that young students are the heaviest internet users – practically 100% of them use the internet every day – we decided

[25] Initially, we intended to obtain around 500 completed questionnaires, but, as we said, we received only 229.

to organize a focus group, which took place on 31 December 2014 at the University of Beira Interior (UBI). Ten students participated in the focus group, and was formed of participants of both genders from the undergraduate and graduate courses in Communication Sciences at UBI.

The session, which was videotaped and observed by one of our PhD students, focused on five main issues: the concept of political participation, the relationship between the political parties and the citizens, forms of political communication, the position of political parties regarding communication, and the internet and social networks as means of political communication. Next, we highlight the main conclusions for each of these topics.

The concept of political participation

The general opinion was that political participation goes far beyond the simple act of voting. The technologies are seen as facilitators, leading one participant to say "currently, the only people not taking part are those who don't want to". Access to information is the core element. One participant raised the hypothesis of education for citizenship. There was a clear perspective of criticism of a certain apoliticism, namely in other social groups, which are perceived as being uninterested in political and civic life.

The relationship between the political parties and the citizens

A critical discussion emerged about the explicit and/or implicit idea of a confrontation between generations and the power of education. One participant alerted to the fact that politicians use inaccessible language: "They speak to people who cannot understand". It is a communication strategy, favouring form over function, and overlapping to form the content. Individual responsibility in shaping policy was also emphasized. That is, it is up to citizens to seek information.

The forms of political communication

According to some of the participants, communication strategies should focus on interpersonal communication. New technologies were criticized because they are impersonal and it is not always possible to get feedback. Interpersonal communication should be prioritized, but the costs are enormous. Some participants, from courses such as engineering, politically think like older people. The politicization of young students often emerges when searching for their first job.

The position of political parties in regard to communication

The causes of the gap between citizens and their political representatives lie in the fact that party organizations close in on themselves, using language that is inaccessible to ordinary citizens. The platforms are seen as something approaching one-way only communication. According to various participants, today one type of use based on "disclosure" is dominant. There is no real dialogue. The figure and leadership are seen as prevailing over platforms that people can use.

Internet and social networks as means of political communication

Politics are designed as a continuous process. There was some criticism about each individual's capacity to mobilize: "Nobody moves. There is a great deal of conformity". Again, the dilemma of finding information emerges and with it something that is underlying the principle of "self-responsibility" for the purposes of mobilization and political and civic participation.

Discussion and conclusions

At this time, we must ask ourselves if and how our research data allows us to answer our research questions and validate our hypotheses – and, finally, to give an answer to our research problem. Let us begin with our research questions (RQ) and hypotheses (H).

Research questions

As we said in a previous section, our research problem was: What is the degree of correspondence between the participation that the websites of the Portuguese political parties allow citizens and citizens' expectations about their participation – in non-electoral periods? From this general problem, we derived three research questions, which we discuss below.

RQ1. What are the participatory tools available to citizens on the Portuguese political parties' websites? How do Portuguese political parties interact with citizens via the participatory internet tools available on their websites?

Our content analysis of the participatory tools showed that the adequacy score of all websites exceed 50%, while the overall average was 63.5%, with presence-variety scoring 52.9%, visibility 62.6%, and functionality 75%. More specifically:

Presence: regarding the eight participatory tools, all the websites included contact details, suggestions and social media. However, Facebook, surely the most important social network at the moment, was not found on the websites of the PCP and the CDS/PP. Four websites had comments and RSS syndication (Comments: PSD, CDS-PP, BE, PS; RSS: CDS-PP, PCP, BE, PS). Only one website (PS) had a forum/chat facility. None of the websites included a blog.

Visibility: Social media was the most common and most visible interactive tool, but the scores of the others tools were also very satisfactory (as we said, the average was 62.6%).

Functionality: The websites were ranked higher for functionality, because they are generally clear and simple to use, although their visibility could be significantly improved.

Therefore, in terms of the presence, visibility and functionality of the participatory tools, the websites seemed to be quite good. The problems began when we tried to use those tools to interact with the political parties. As we saw in our analyses of the Facebook pages (of the BE, PS and PSD) and our interaction experiment – and as confirmed by the interviews and the survey – the parties do not pursue interaction. Whether this is because they do not have enough resources, or because they do not want to lose control of the message, the parties only *appear* to be open to interaction; in reality, they do not join online conversations. Dialogue, when it takes place, is not between the party and citizens (commenters), but among the citizens (commenters) themselves. Therefore, in spite of participatory internet tools being present on political parties' websites, few dialogic features are really implemented.

RQ2. What is the opinion of the leaders of Portuguese political parties and the communication managers about the citizens' participation on their websites? Does this participation involve any change to the political party agenda (themes, actions)?

As mentioned previously, it was not possible to interview the leaders of the parties, but only the communication managers; all five interviews were done face-to-face and were more or less exhaustive (we must publicly thank the political parties for their openness and cooperation with our research project).

Communication managers tend to see websites more as instruments of disintermediation, a channel to disseminate their messages directly to citizens without the filters of the mass media. This allow the parties not only to tell their own story, but also to provide the media and journalists with the information they need to tell their stories about the parties, their leaders and actions. As had been proven by several other studies in other countries, the function of providing information takes priority over promoting interaction on political parties' websites. This also happens because, as the communication managers acknowledge, dealing with citizens' participation on the parties' websites is seen to be an almost impossible task, given the time and human resources it would need ("an army behind the machine", as one of them says); the parties are unable to manage it. However, citizens' participation on the websites is seen to be very important, because it allows parties to observe and monitor what people think about several political issues and the respective proposals put forward by the parties.

The difficulty in dealing with citizens' participation on their websites is, surely, one of the main things preventing parties from using the contributions brought by that participation to introduce changes to their political agendas (themes, actions) – with the notable exception of the CDS/PP, whose communication manager explicitly says that his party has integrated some of citizens' proposals in the past.

RQ3. What are citizens' opinions about the possibility of entering into interaction with parties via their websites? How do they evaluate their own participation on the websites?

As our survey showed, most of the respondents (79.91%) say they do not visit – and so do not interact with – the political parties' websites; only an average of 26.53% of the visitors visit the parties' websites at least one day a week – which means 5.32% of our sample, i.e. 12 people in 229. Besides that, we should keep in mind that these numbers do not represent all Portuguese citizens, but only those who have and use the internet, as was the case with our respondents. In fact, as we saw in a previous point of this report, at the end of 2014, only 65% of Portuguese citizens aged between 16 and 74 accessed the internet – which means that 35% did not use it.

Therefore, in spite of all the interactive tools that parties' websites provide them with, citizens do not seem very interested in interacting. Those who do not visit – or interact with – the political parties' websites mainly do not do so because they have no interest in politics, distrust the information provided by the websites, or distrust politics in general.

And, as we have seen, parties also do not seem very interested in interacting with citizens – a result that is confirmed by the interaction experiment, the interviews and the survey. Both citizens and the political parties seem more interested in the issue of getting or providing information, not interaction. However, both citizens and political parties think that parties' websites are important as a means of communication between parties and citizens: for the citizens, to access direct political information about the parties; for the parties, to monitor citizens' opinions about them and the political issues at stake.

Hypotheses

We set the general hypothesis that there is a lack of correspondence between the participation the Portuguese political parties' websites allow citizens and citizens' expectations about it. Regarding our more specific research questions, we defined three hypotheses, the validation of which we discuss next. We shall return to our general hypothesis afterwards.

H1. Citizens' participation tends to favour image-based forms of expression (videos, photos), is predominantly supportive (not critical) of the political party, and tends not to depend on the political-ideological orientation of the party.

Our research only partially validated this hypothesis.

Regarding forms of expression, our content analysis of Facebook showed that citizens cannot make posts, only comments using the written word; in our survey, citizens say that the forms of participation they use the most are e-mailing the party, participating on social media (liking, sharing, etc.), and making comments – sending pictures and uploading videos are minority activities (4.04% and 1.01% of respondents respectively). This result is surely also explained by the fact that parties tend to monitor the use of photos and videos both on their websites and on their social networks – since, as our content analysis of Facebook showed, an amount of 84.09% political party posts included a type of image, while 15.91% had only text. Image-based forms of expression existed, therefore, but were used by parties, not citizens.

As regards the statement that citizens' participation tends to be predominantly supportive (not critical) of the political party, the results of our content analysis of Facebook shows that, with the exception of the PSD (the leading government party), the comments are more favourable than unfavourable or neutral, which may lead us to conclude that the participants are mostly members or supporters of the political parties.

In terms of ideology, since all the posts were authored by the political parties, we can only consider Likes, Comments and Shares. The order of the parties is as follows (from the first to third place): Likes – PS – BE – PSD; Comments – PS – PSD – BE; Shares – PS – BE – PSD. We can therefore conclude that there tends to be more participation on the websites of the parties of the left, especially the PS, than on those of the centre-right parties. The PS' first position is also verified by our survey, in which the most respondents that say they are members or supporters of a political party and visit its website belong to the PS (10 in 46 and 20 in 46 respectively).

H2. The leaders of the parties and the people responsible for the management of their websites tend to see citizen participation more as an instrument of delivering their own message than as a way of listening to citizens' messages.

This hypothesis undoubtedly highlights one of the most important results of the interviews with the political parties' communication managers. In fact, the political parties see their websites mostly as a tool of "disintermediation", i.e. a means of reaching citizens directly, bypassing the traditional media gatekeepers. In this process, citizens are not heard but are monitored: parties are interested not in answering citizens' questions, comments and suggestions but in observing what citizens think and say about their initiatives and proposals – perhaps in order to adapt them to citizens' perspectives. Therefore, citizens' "participation" on the parties' websites is seen by parties as merely instrumental; it is not real participation, but participation that can add to (and change) something.

This result of the interviews is fully corroborated by the results of the Facebook content analysis, the interaction experiment, and the survey. As we said before, the content analysis showed that citizens can comment on the posts made by the parties and on other citizens' comments, but cannot post themselves; the interaction experiment showed that citizens hardly get answers from the political parties; the survey showed that citizens say parties mostly never or only sometimes answer them (45.65% and 36.96% respectively, i.e. in 82.61% of cases).

H3. The citizens expect the websites of the political parties to be more open (with fewer constraints) to their participation, and to have more of an impact on the agenda and plans of the political parties.

Apparently, our survey did not validate this hypothesis. In fact, as we have already said, when we asked citizens about their reasons for visiting the political parties' websites, they did not mention the lack of openness of those means of communication, but rather their own disinterest in politics, their preference for receiving political information through the traditional media (also because they consider websites to be propagandistic and biased), and even their distrust in politics. Besides that, most citizens in our sample that visit the parties' websites consider them to be a useful or very useful (45.65% and 23.91% respectively, i.e. a total of 69.56%) means of communication with citizens.

However, when asked about the usefulness of the websites, citizens mention citizens' political participation/the exercise of citizenship in last place (5.13% of the sample), while obtaining information or getting more in-depth information about the political parties, and encouraging closer contact and more direct communication with the parties are mentioned as the two first reasons.

It therefore seems that citizens are not really worried about the websites' possible lack of openness to their participation, for the simple reason that they are not interested in participating more than they already do. This is where there seems to be an example of what, inverting the famous expression by Pippa Norris (2000), we could call the "vicious circle" of participation: citizens do not participate because political parties do not allow them to do so; but when political parties do allow them to participate, citizens do not. One of the possible explanations of this circle could be the fact that citizens do not participate because they do not see any real effects from their participation, that is, the participation political parties' websites allow them is not real participation, in the sense that they can exert some influence on the political parties' agenda.

Research problem

Let us return, now, to our project's research problem: What is the degree of correspondence between the participation that the websites of the Portuguese political parties allow citizens and citizens' expectations about their participation – in non-electoral periods?

To summarize, and if we bear in mind what has been said up to now, the obvious answer to the problem/question would be a short, affirmative one: there is a degree of total correspondence. However, this short, affirmative answer hides a doubly negative one: i) the political parties' websites *do not* provide citizens with real participation, but only a simulation of participation, with persuasive and propagandistic objectives; ii) citizens *do not* expect the political parties' websites to allow them more participation than they already do, since what citizens mainly want from the websites is information about the parties. The problem therefore lies elsewhere.

Web 2.0 has created tools that can potentially foster dialogue between citizens and democratic institutions, namely political parties. However, once again, technology does not have the final word, since political dialogue is mainly a question of civic and political culture, both for citizens and political parties.

This culture implies that, on their side, political parties really want to listen to citizens, to their proposals and suggestions, and try to incorporate those proposals and suggestions into their plans, thereby transcending the idea of "just talking" about the need for citizen participation. This requires, of course, greater investment in financial, technological and human resources to avoid a situation in which, to use a metaphor, political parties have a Formula 1 car that they drive like a cart, i.e. that they do not use effectively. This can only lead to a discrediting of politics and the political parties themselves.

On the other hand, citizens need to think that online participation is only one form of political participation, and that it does not substitute other, direct forms of participation. Sending an email to a party representative or signing an online petition are important things, but their effect is limited. Voting, participating in a meeting, protesting, attending a demonstration or rally, boycotting a product, to give only a few examples, are also important forms of political participation, which the forms of online participation should be seen to complement.

What is the critical word? The critical word, we believe, is not technology but *education*. In fact, of all human actions, education is surely the most political one. It is just for this reason that the first important philosophical work on politics was, at the same time, the first important philosophical work on education – we mean, of course, Plato's *Republic* (*Politeia*). In this work, dedicated to defining justice, Plato describes not only the ideal community, but also the education of men (namely the "Guardians") that is necessary to build that community. Even if we do not agree with most of Plato's theses, what we want to stress here is his intuition about the link between politics and education – a link that was also stressed by contemporary philosophers such as John Dewey and Hannah Arendt, to cite only two (whose theses we also do not fully agree with).

The education we talk about is education for a democratic, pluralistic society. It cannot be confused with ideological indoctrination or with training for any kind of "horse race". It should be based on the universal values of freedom and respect for the human person, and proceduralist and deliberative in the sense proposed by Habermas (1994).

Appendix 1

Interview questions

1. What are the main objectives behind the creation and development of your party's website?
2. Do you consider the party website to be a favoured means of achieving interaction and fostering citizen participation? Why?
3. In your opinion, do citizens often interact with the political party through the participatory tools provided by the website (e.g. e-mail, chat, forum, etc.)?
4. How do you evaluate the party's response to comments and other forms of citizen participation on the website? Why?
5. How is citizen participation managed on the party's website? Who manages it? How often? Using what means?
6. What are the main difficulties encountered in managing citizens' participation on the party's website? Why?
7. There is a link to social networks, e.g. Facebook, available on the party's website. Is there a specific strategy for managing and monitoring comments made on social networks?
8. Does the party's agenda include citizens' participation on the website? If so, in what ways?

Appendix 2

Questionnaire

A. CHARACTERISTICS OF THE RESPONDENT

1. Sex:
1.1. Male
1.2. Female
1.3. Other
1.4. No answer

2. Age (on 31 December 2014):
2.1. Under 18
2.2. 18 to 35
2.3. 36 to 50
2.4. 51 to 65
2.5. Over 66
2.6. No answer

3. Education level:
3.1. None
3.2. Year 4
3.3. Year 6
3.4. Year 9
3.5. Year 12
3.6. Bachelor's degree
3.7. Master's degree
3.8. PhD
3.9. No answer

4. Marital status:
4.1. Single
4.2. Married
4.3. Non-marital partnership
4.4. Widow(er)
4.5. Separated/divorced
4.6. No answer

5. Number of members of the household (including the respondent):
5.1. 1 member
5.2. 2 members
5.3. 3 members

5.4. 4 members
5.5. 5 or more members
5.6. No answer

6. Region of residence (Portugal):
6.1. North
6.2. Centre
6.3. Lisbon
6.4. Alentejo
6.5. Algarve
6.6. Madeira
6.7. Azores
6.8. Abroad
6.9. No answer

7. City and county of residence: ________________

8. Employment status:
8.1. Employee in the private sector
8.2. Employee in the public sector
8.3. Self-employed/entrepreneur
8.4. Student
8.5. Unemployed
8.6. Retired
8.7. Other
8.8. No answer

9. Professional area (if retired or unemployed, refer to your last profession):
9.1. Senior manager in public or private sector
9.2. Specialist in an intellectual or scientific profession
9.3. Mid-level technical or professional staff
9.4. Administrative staff or similar
9.5. Service staff or salesperson
9.6. Farmer or skilled worker in agriculture or fisheries
9.7. Worker, craftsman or similar worker
9.8. Facilities or equipment operator or assembly worker
9.9. Unqualified worker
9.10. No answer

10. Indicate your personal net income (average per month in euros):
10.1. Up to €500

10.2. Between €501 and €1000
10.3. Between €1001 and €1500
10.4. Between €1501 and €2000
10.5. Over €2000
10.6. No answer

11. Do you have a computer at home:
11.1. Yes
11.2. No
11.3. No answer
11.1. If you answered yes, please give the type of computer (you can indicate several types):
11.1.1. Desktop
11.1.2. Laptop
11.1.3. Tablet/Palmtop
11.1.4. Other
11.1.5. No answer

12. What kind of internet connection do you have at home:
12.1. Broadband (cable, ADSL, wireless, 4G, etc.)
12.2. Narrowband (analogue line, ISDN, 3G, etc.)
12. 3. Don't know
12.4. None
12.5. No answer

13. How often do you use the internet?:
13.1. Don't use it
13.2. One day a week
13.3. Several days a week
13.4. Every day
13.5. No answer

14. Place where you usually use the internet (you can indicate more than one location):
14.1. Home
14.1. Work/study
14.1. Public places
14.1. Other
14.1. No answer

15. Membership of a political party:
15.1. None
15.2. BE

15.3. PCP
15.4. PS
15.5. PSD
15.6 .CDS/PP
15.7. Other
15.8. No answer

16. Support for a political party:
16.1. None
16.2. BE
16.3. PCP
16.4. PS
16.5. PSD
16.6. CDS/PP
16.7. Other
16.8. No answer

17. Do you usually use the internet to visit / browse websites of political parties':
17.1. Yes
17.2. No
17.3. No answer
17.4. Please give the reason for your answer: _______________
If you answered No, your questionnaire ENDS HERE.
If yes, please answer the questions in Part B, below.

B. PARTICIPATION ON POLITICAL PARTIES' WEBSITES

18. Frequency of visits to the political parties' websites (you may indicate more than one):

	1. Never	2. Rarely	3. One day a week	4. Several days a week	5. Every day	6. No answer
18.1. BE						
18.2. PCP						
18.3. PS						
18.4. PSD						
18.5. CDS/PP						
18.6. Other						

19. Have you visited a political party's website in order to do one of the following actions (you may indicate more than one):

19.1. Send an email
19.2. Send photos
19.3. Send videos
19.4. Make suggestions
19.5. Make comments
19.6. Participate on social networks (Facebook, etc.)
19.7. Participate in chats
19.8. Participate in forums
19.9. Volunteer for party actions (meetings, rallies, etc.)
19.10. Make donations
19.11. Join the party
19.12. Other

20. Did the parties respond to your participation on their websites?

20.1. Never
20.2. Sometimes
20.3. Often
20.4. Always
20.5. No answer

21. If the parties responded to your participation on their websites, indicate the medium used (you may indicate more than one):

21.1. E-mail
21.2. Answer to your comment on a news story

21.3. Answer to your comment on a post
21.4. Answer to your suggestion
21.5. Other

22. Which political parties' Facebook pages have you already visited? (You may indicate more than one)
22.1. BE
22.2. PCP
22.3. PS
22.4. PSD
22.5. CDS / PP
22.6. Other

23. Do you usually share or comment on news you read on the parties' websites through social networks (e.g. Facebook)?
23.1. Yes
23.2. No

24. Please rate the usefulness of the political parties' websites as a means of communication with citizens according to the following scale:
24.1. Not very useful
24.2. Somewhat useful
24.3. Useful
24.4. Very useful

25. Please justify your answer:

____

____

Appendix 3

Socio-demography of the respondents of the survey

Gender	Number	Per cent
Male	111	48.47%
Female	118	51.53%
Other	0	0%
No answer	0	0%
Total	229	100%

Table 7.10: Gender

	Number	Per cent
Under 18	0	0%
18 to 35	76	33.19%
36 to 50	120	52.40%
51 to 65	29	12.66%
Over 66	4	1.75%
No answer	0	0%
Total	229	100%

Table 7.11: Age

	Number	Per cent
None	0	0%
Year 5	0	0%
Year 6	1	0.44%
Year 9	2	0.87%
Year 12	16	6.99%
Bachelor's degree	63	27.51%
Master's	62	27.07%
PhD	85	37.12%
No answer	0	0%
Total	229	100%

Table 7.12: Education (highest education level completed)

Marital Status	Number	Per cent
Single	76	33.19%
Married	103	44.98%
Non-marital partnership	24	10.48%
Widow(er)	0	0%
Separated/divorced	26	11.35%
No answer	0	0%
Total	229	100%

Table 7.13: Marital status

	Number	Per cent
1 member	46	20.09%
2 members	54	23.58%
3 members	55	24.02%
4 members	63	27.51%
5 or more members	11	4.80%
No answer	0	0%
Total	247	100%

Table 7.14: Number of members of the household (including the respondent)

	Number	Per cent
North	73	31.88%
Centre	89	38.86%
Lisbon	38	16.59%
Alentejo	13	5.68%
Algarve	5 2.	2.18%
Madeira	1	0.44%
Azores	2	0.87%
Abroad	8	3.49%
No answer	0	0%
Total	229	100%

Table 7.15: Region of residence (Portugal)

	Number	Per cent
Employee in the private sector	34	14.85%
Employee in the public sector	131	57.21%
Self-employed/entrepreneur	11	4.80%
Student	25	10.92%
Unemployed	10	4.37%
Retired	4	1.75%
Other	14	6.11%
No answer	0	0%
Total	229	100%

Table 7.16: Employment status

	Number	Per cent
Senior manager in public or private sector	44	19.21%
Specialist in an intellectual or scientific profession	126	55.02%
Mid-level technical or professional staff	26	11.35%
Administrative staff or similar	13	5.68%
Service staff or salesperson	6	2.62%
Farmer or skilled worker in agriculture or fisheries	2	0.87%
Worker, craftsman or similar worker	0	0%
Facilities or equipment operator or assembly worker	1	0.44%
Unqualified worker	11	4.80%
No answer	0	0%
Total	229	100%

Table 7.17: Professional Area

	Number	Per cent
Up to €500	37	16.16%
Between € 501 and €1000	42	18.34%
Between €1001 and €1500	57	24.89%
Between €1501 and € 2000	67	29.26%
Over €2000	26	11.35%
No answer	0	0%
Total	229	100%

Table 7.18: Personal net income (average per month in euros)

	Number	Per cent
Yes	229	100%
No	0	0%
No answer	0	0%
Total	229	100%

Table 7.19: Computer at home

	Number	Per cent
Desktop	67	29.26%
Laptop	210	91.70%
Tablet/palmtop	83	36.24%
Other type	8	3.49%
No answer	0	0%

Table 7.20: Type of computer at home (multiple answers)

	Number	Per cent
Broadband (cable, ADSL, wireless, 4G, etc.)	217	94.76%
Narrowband (analogue line, ISDN, 3G, etc.)	7	3.06%
Don't know	5	2.18%
None	0	0%
No answer	0	0%
Total	229	100%

Table 7.21: Internet connection type at home

	Number	Per cent
Don't use it	0	0%
One day a week	5	2.18%
Several days a week	12	5.24%
Every day	212	92.58%
No answer	0	0%
Total	229	100%

Table 7.22: Internet usage frequency

	Number	Per cent
Home	223	97.38%
Work/study	200	87.34%
Public places	119	51.97%
Other	19	8.30%
No answer	0	0%

Table 7.23: Place where internet usually used (multiple answer)

	Number	Per cent
None	205	89.52%
BE	4	1.75%
PCP	0	0%
PS	14	6.11%
PSD	1	0.44%
CDS/PP	2	0.87%
Other	3	1.31%
No answer	0	0%
Total	229	100%

Table 7.24: Membership of a political party

	Number	Per cent
None	112	48.91%
BE	17	7.42%
PCP	12	5.24%
PS	53	23.14%
PSD	17	7.42%
CDS/PP	6	2.62%
Other	12	5.24%
No answer	0	0%
Total	229	100%

Table 7.25: Support for a political party

	Number	Per cent
Yes	46	20.09%
No	183	79.91%
No answer	0	0%
Total	229	100%

Table 7.26: Internet usage for visiting/surfing political parties' websites

Bibliography

Belchior, A. M. & Freire, A. (2012). Is party type relevant to an explanation of policy congruence? Catchall versus ideological parties in the Portuguese case. *International Political Science Review*, 34 (3): 273–288.

Cardoso, G.; Cunha, C. & Nascimento, S. (2003). O parlamento português na construção de uma democracia digital. *Sociologia, Problemas e Práticas*, 42: 113-140.

Cardoso, G.; Mendonça, S.; Lima, T.; Paisana, M. & Neves, M, (2014). *A internet em Portugal: sociedade em rede 2014*. Lisbon: Obercom.

Carpentier, N. (2011). The concept of participation. If they have access and interact, do they really participate?. *CM, Communication Management Quarterly/Casopis Za Upravljanje Komuniciranjem*, 6 (21): 13-36.

Dahlgren, P. (2011). Parameters of online participation: conceptualising civic contingencies. *CM, Communication Management Quarterly/Casopis Za Upravljanje Komuniciranjem*, 6 (21): 87-110.

Deacon, D.; Pickering, M.; Golding, P. & Murdock, G. (2007). *Researching communications: a practical guide to methods in media and cultural analysis* (2nd Ed.). London: Hodder Arnold.

Denzin, N. K. (1970). *The research act in sociology*. Chicago: Aldine.

Gibson. R. K.; Margolis, M.; Resnick, D. & Ward, S. (2003). Election campaigning on the WWW in the US and UK: a comparative analysis. *Party Politics*, 9 (1): 47-75.

Gomes, W.; Fernandes, B.; Reis, L. & Silva, T. (2009). "Politics 2,0": a campanha on-line de Barack Obama em 2008. *Revista de Sociologia e Política*, 17 (34): 29-43.

Habermas, J. (1989). *The structural transformation of the public sphere: an inquiry into a category of bourgeois society*. Cambridge: Polity Press.

Habermas, J. (1994). Three normative models of democracy. *Constellations*, 1 (1), 1-10.

INE-Instituto Nacional de Estatística (2014, November 6). *Sociedade da informação e do conhecimento – Inquérito à utilização de tecnologias da informação e da comunicação pelas famílias 2014 (Destaque – informação à comunicação social)*. Lisbon: Author. Available at: https://www.ine.pt/xportal/xmain?xpid=INE&xpgid=ine_destaques&DESTAQUESdest_boui=211422735&DESTAQUESmodo=2

Kirchheimer, O. (1966). The transformation of western european party systems. In J. Lapalombara & M. Weiner (Eds.), *Political parties and political development* (pp. 177-200). Princeton: Princeton University Press.

López del Ramo, J. (2014). Type, visibility and functioning of participatory resources on the websites of portuguese political parties: a preliminary analysis. In P. Serra, E. Camilo & G. Gonçalves (Eds.), *Political participation and web 2.0* (pp. 243-272). Covilhã: Labcom Books.

Norris, P. (2000). *A virtuous circle: political communications in post-industrial societies*. New York: Cambridge University Press.

Rodrigues, R. I. (2015). *Comunicação política 2.0 em Portugal: estratégias on-line na campanha eleitoral para as legislativas 2009* (Unpublished doctoral dissertation). Covilhã: University of Beira Interior.

Rolfe, M. J. (2008). From big to little screens: recurring images of democratic credibility and the net. *Scan*, 5: 1–12. Available at: http://scan.net.au/scan/journal/display.php?journal_id=110

Schweitzer, E. J. (2005), Election campaigning online: German party websites in the 2002 national elections. *European Journal of Communication*, 20 (3): 327–351.

Serra, J. P. (2012). Novos media e participação política. *Observatorio (OBS*) Journal*, 6 (2): 127-155.

Serra, P.; Fidalgo, A.; Gradim, A.; Sousa, A.; Camilo, E.; Gonçalves, G.; Ferreira, I.; Canavilhas, J.; Rodrigues, R. & Cunha, T. C. (2014). The research project "New media and political participation". In P. Serra, E. Camilo & G. Gonçalves (Eds.), *Political participation and web 2.0* (pp. 5-16). Covilhã: Labcom Books.

Silva, C. I. P. (2012). *A comunicação partidária online: os websites num contexto não eleitoral* (Unpublished master's dissertation). Aveiro: Universidade de Aveiro.

Smith, A., & Rainie, L. (2008). *The internet and the 2008 election*. Pew Internet & American Life Project. Available at: `http://www.pewinternet.org/Reports/2008/The-Internet-and-the-2008-Election.aspx`

Smith, A. (2009), *The internet's role in campaign 2008*. Pew Internet & American Life Project. Available at: `http://www.pewinternet.org/Reports/2009/6--The-Internets-Role-in-Campaign-2008.aspx`

Strom, K. (1999). A behavioral theory of competitive political parties. *American Journal of Political Science*, 34 (2): 565-598.

Index

www.ingramcontent.com/pod-product-compliance
Lightning Source LLC
Chambersburg PA
CBHW072133020426
42334CB00018B/1776